The Child Carer's
HANDBOOK

the last date below.

The Child Carer's
HANDBOOK
A Guide to Everyday Needs, Difficulties and Disorders

Lorraine Wickham

Hodder Arnold

A MEMBER OF THE HODDER HEADLINE GROUP

Orders: please contact Bookpoint Ltd, 130 Milton Park, Abingdon, Oxon OX14 4SB.
Telephone: 44 (0)1235 827720. Fax: 44 (0)1235 400454. Lines are open 9.00–6.00, Monday to
Saturday, with a 24-hour message answering service. You can also order through our website
www.hoddereducation.co.uk

If you have any comments to make about this, or any of our other titles, please send them to
educationenquiries@hodder.co.uk

British Library Cataloguing in Publication Data
A catalogue record for this title is available from the British Library

ISBN-10: 0 340 91234 0
ISBN-13: 978 0 340 91234 8

This Edition Published 2006
Impression number 10 9 8 7 6 5 4 3 2 1
Year 2009 2008 2007 2006

The contents of this handbook are for information only. Advice should always be sought directly from
those who are properly trained and qualified and any actions taken should be under the supervision of
the appropriate professional.

Hodder Headline's policy is to use papers that are natural, renewable and recyclable products and made
from wood grown in sustainable forests. The logging and manufacturing processes are expected to
conform to the environmental regulations of the country of origin.

Cover photo © Camille Tokerud/The Image Bank/Getty Images

Typeset by Dorchester Typesetting Group Ltd
Printed in Great Britain for Hodder Arnold, an imprint of Hodder Education, a member of the Hodder
Headline Group, 338 Euston Road, London NW1 3BH by CPI Bath

Contents

Preface

All of us in the company and care of children sooner or later come across those with illnesses or other difficulties which require particular understanding. As parents, students, childcare workers, teachers, as well as a host of allied professionals (psychologists, speech and language therapists, and so on), at some time we find ourselves asking, 'What is that?' 'What should I do?' 'How can I help?'

It may not be essential to know all the ins and outs, but it is important to have some insight. It may be necessary to administer medication, or to be on the lookout for side effects or allergic reactions; it may also be the case that the situation has to be explained to parents, or provision made for special aids.

The fact is that no one can be an expert in all things, and, realistically speaking, it is not necessary, since there are experts in most fields to whom we can refer. However, I have become increasingly aware of a need for a quick, reliable point of reference, which gives the basics at a glance and provides suggestions on how to find out more if necessary.

That is what this handbook is about – providing you with basic information, quickly and accurately.

The handbook is eclectic, describing a range of fairly common needs that children might have in different situations, as well as defining various terms, labels and what some might call 'jargon' linked to these needs. The entries run alphabetically and most contain cross-references to other entries or to a glossary of simple definitions. Terms in italics in *CAPITAL LETTERS* indicate a full entry on that topic. Terms in **bold** direct you to the glossary. In addition, most entries include website addresses, to help you begin the search for additional information.

Any data and survey information cited are mostly UK-based and, as such, may not reflect the situation in other countries. However, many of the websites which I have found informative contain links to similar sites in other countries, and it would be a relatively simple process to access country-specific data. The websites referred to are those that I have found useful, but I have tried to be cautious and objective at all times.

The contents of this handbook are for information only. None of the entries or sources imply my approval, disapproval or endorsement; nor should any information be taken as legal, medical or any other kind of advice on my part. Advice should always be sought directly from those who are properly trained and qualified, and any actions taken should be under the supervision of the appropriate professionals.

This guide is quite simply the synthesis of many years as a child carer and educator in mainstream and specialised settings, in several different countries. It is the book I always wished I had had on my bookshelf or in my desk drawer.

Acknowledgements

Many children and child carers are the source of this handbook, and I acknowledge each and every one of them. I particularly value my time at the Autistic Children's Centre in South Australia and the years in Italy.

My special thanks go to Chris, Kay, Shirin and Val for thinking that this book was more than a good idea and saying so, to Emma and Jo and all at Hodder for their enthusiasm and professional guidance and to Ali (and Amy) for the hours of reading, re-reading, playing devil's advocate and encouragement.

For Ali, for mum, for children and for those who care.

➤➤ Adenoids

The adenoids are a small mass of tissue at the back of the nose (see figure 1). The tissue is composed mainly of lymphocytes (white blood cells involved in the production of **antibodies**, proteins which help the body fight infection). The adenoids are present in all infants and children, start regressing just before puberty and are usually absent in adults.

adenoids

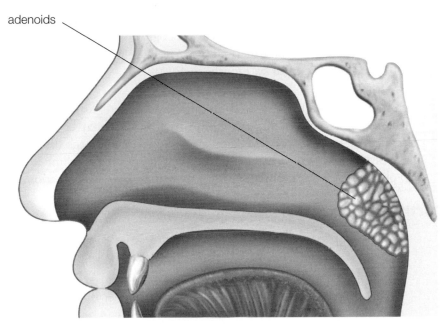

Fig 1 ▲ Diagram of Adenoids

If the adenoids become persistently enlarged and/or infected they may need surgical removal (adenoidectomy). Research indicates no effects on the **immune system** when the adenoids are removed. It is thought that some years ago the adenoids served a significant defence function against various childhood *INFECTIONS* that are no longer common (e.g. parasites, worms), and that they are no longer effective against the range of infections that occur in a modern urban population.

Enlarged/infected adenoids can cause snoring, apnoea (blockage of breathing for a few seconds at a time during sleep), ear infections, reduction of smell and taste, tiredness related to poor sleeping, poor concentration at school, absence from school due to infections, prolonged use of *ANTIBIOTICS*, open-mouthed breathing, drooling, sinus infections and headaches, poor hearing accuracy, possible hearing loss and speech difficulties (e.g. poor articulation – the clear production of speech sounds).

1

Treatment

There are three possibilities: medication, time and surgical removal of the adenoids.

1 Medication

   Nasal sprays can reduce enlarged adenoids.

2 Time

   Enlarged adenoids can reduce naturally over time. However, blockage of the adenoidal area (cheeks, eyes, nose, etc.) can affect facial or dental development; chronic poor sleeping can affect growth and learning; two or three infections per year associated with ear fluid mean that hearing may be decreased for up to six months each year.

3 Surgical removal of the adenoids

   The procedure typically takes 5–15 minutes to complete, usually under general anaesthesia. After surgery, mild pain medication may be prescribed – a few children will complain of a stiff or sore neck (due to some stress to the neck muscles) – and some activities may be limited (e.g. playing outdoors, swimming) for a short time after the operation.

Further information

American Academy of Otolaryngology – Head and Neck Surgery, www.entnet.org/healthinfo (look under Pediatric) (accessed 20 September 2005)

▶▶ Adoption

Adoption is a legal procedure in which all parental rights and responsibilities are transferred from the birth parent/s to the adopters. Adoption becomes legal after the child has lived with the adopters for at least 13 weeks.

Some children cannot be cared for adequately by their birth parents; some are orphaned by the death of one or both parents; and some are abused and/or neglected and removed from the birth family.

Children come from a great variety of backgrounds: many are of school age and some are groups of brothers and sisters who need to be placed together. Many will have experienced several changes of home and carers, and the resulting uncertainty and insecurity may produce some challenging behaviours.

In the UK in 2003 there were 5354 registered adoptions, of which 4 per cent were children under the age of 1; 46 per cent were aged 1–4; 32 per cent were aged 5–9; 14 per cent were aged 10–14; and 4 per cent were aged 15–17.

Should children be told that they are adopted? The consensus is yes, and that adoptive parents should give the child age-appropriate information as early as possible.

Contact with the birth family

Rules and regulations can vary according to country, state, and so on, but contact of varying kinds is generally possible; for example, periodic exchange of written information via the adoption agency, and even arrangements for a child to have direct contact with the birth family, including grandparents and siblings placed elsewhere, and sometimes with birth parent/s.

Legal arrangements can vary regarding tracing birth parents. For example, in England, Wales and Northern Ireland, adopted children have the right to see their original birth certificate when they are 18, while in Scotland the age is 16. Some adoptees are satisfied with knowing that the contact opportunity is there, while others have a strong desire to trace their birth parent/s and/or other birth family members.

Potential problems

✦ Feelings of being abandoned, sadness, depression, low **self-image**.
✦ Being teased or suffering from *BULLYING*.
✦ Anger, resentment, rebelliousness (directed at adoptive parents in the absence of birth parent/s).

3

✦ Resentment of adoptive siblings.
✦ Special talents and/or special needs inherited from birth parents can go unrecognised or undervalued in the adoptive family.
✦ Obsessive searching for birth parent/s.

Telling childcare workers, classroom teachers or other professionals that a child is adopted can be very positive, especially if there are particular issues or needs that they should be sensitive towards, or support strategies that they can provide or be involved with.

Further information

British Association for Adoption and Fostering, www.baaf.org.uk (accessed 20 September 2005)

▶▶ Aggression and non-compliance

These behaviours should be considered in the light of **developmental stages** and the child's social and emotional environment. Certain behaviours are typical of a particular developmental stage (e.g. defiance during the 'terrible twos'), and a child under stress is more likely to behave badly than a child who is relaxed. A child who is 'allowed' to behave a certain way believes that there is nothing wrong with his/her behaviour. Some children are in *TEMPERAMENT* more volatile, restless and impulsive. Some children have significant social, emotional and/or learning difficulties underlying their behaviour (e.g. *DEPRESSION, ATTENTION DEFICIT DISORDERS, AUTISM*).

Aggression and non-compliance and other antisocial behaviour is more common in boys and it can occur at home and/or in other settings (e.g. day-care).

Aggression may take any of the following forms:
+ *BULLYING*
+ destructive behaviour
+ hitting, pinching, etc.
+ lashing out
+ shouting, swearing
+ temper tantrums
+ throwing things.

Non-compliance can mean the child ignores adult requests, or simply refuses to do anything that s/he is asked.

Evaluating the problem

+ Home environment: parents' relationship, behaviours, health (physical and mental), expectations; traumatic events that have upset the child and/or other family members (e.g. new baby, loss of income).
+ Family history: similar problems for parents or other relatives; mental illness.
+ Developmental history: infant behaviours (irritability, poor sleeper); developmental milestones (late talker, clumsy); health (**ear infections**, *ALLERGIES*); reactions to change; present skills, behaviours, etc.

If the information gathered indicates the presence of a physical **impairment** or a social, emotional or learning difficulty, then the child and/or family should be referred to the appropriate support service (e.g. medical specialist,

5

social services, *EDUCATIONAL PSYCHOLOGIST*). If, on the other hand, the problem behaviour appears to be related to adult *BEHAVIOUR MANAGEMENT* styles, then identifying what, where, when, why and how others react is a useful strategy for sorting out the problem.

Management

1   Identify the behaviour as specifically as possible, gathering examples of actual behaviours, such as, 'He hits children when they have a toy he wants', rather than generalised descriptions, such as, 'He's just so aggressive'.
2   When/where does it happen?
3   How do others react when s/he does this (adult reactions, what the child does next)?
4   Evaluate possible reasons for behaviour (as above).
5   Decide on appropriate management (e.g. medical check-up, educational psychologist, *SOCIAL WORKER*, behaviour management programme).

Further information

www.educational-psychologist.co.uk/anger.htm (accessed 20 September 2005)

www.athealth.com (accessed 20 September 2005)

➤➤ Allergies

An allergy is an abnormal reaction or an increased sensitivity to certain substances called **allergen**s. An allergen produces a physical reaction that can range from mild to life-threatening. When the **immune system** is exposed to allergens, it produces **antibodies** that attach themselves to cells in the respiratory and gastrointestinal tracts, skin and blood. These cells release potent chemicals, such as histamine, producing allergic symptoms.

Allergies are more common in children with *ASTHMA* or *ECZEMA*, and certain conditions (e.g. Asthma) can be aggravated by allergies.

Common allergens

Although any environmental material can cause allergies, some are more common than others, including:

✦ Things we breathe in, e.g. pollen from flowers, mould spores, animal fur and saliva, house dust.

✦ Food, e.g. cow's milk, eggs, chicken, shellfish, white fish, peanuts, soybeans, wheat products, chocolate, celery, products containing one or more of these ingredients.

✦ Food additives, e.g. sulphites (used as preservatives), MSG (monosodium glutamate).

✦ Drugs, e.g. *ANTIBIOTICS*, **cortisone**, anti-inflammatories.

✦ Substances which touch the skin, e.g. plant oils, cosmetics and perfumes, nickel in jewellery and close fasteners (zips, buckles), hair dyes, medicinal creams, occupational chemicals (such as bleach or chlorine).

Symptoms

1 Skin

✦ acne-like eruptions

✦ dry, cracked skin, as in eczema

✦ hives

✦ peeling skin

✦ pigmentation (skin colour) changes – may appear as brown or grey blotches

✦ red, itchy rash or blotches

✦ tissue death (necrosis).

2 Respiratory

+ hay fever (rhinitis)
+ Asthma
+ blocked or runny nose
+ coughing
+ laboured breathing, wheezing
+ sneezing.

3 Other

+ low blood pressure
+ nausea and vomiting
+ shock: anaphylactic shock is an acute allergic reaction requiring immediate medical attention (symptoms include: anxiety, itching of the skin, headache, nausea and vomiting, sneezing and coughing, abdominal cramps, hives and swelling of joints and of tissues such as lips, diarrhoea, shortness of breath and wheezing, low blood pressure, convulsions, loss of consciousness)
+ sore joints
+ stomach pains/cramps
+ tongue swelling.

Treatment

+ allergy testing
+ diet and nutrition
+ drugs (e.g. **cortico-steroids**)
+ homeopathy
+ protective clothing for outside
+ remove known allergens from the environment (e.g. chemicals, synthetics in pillows)
+ topical ointments (ointments applied to the skin)
+ **vaccines**.

Further information

My Allergy Net, www.allergy.bravehost.com (accessed 20 September 2005)

www.allergy-guide.net (accessed 20 September 2005)

➤➤ Antibiotics

Antibiotics are medicines that help the body fight bacteria (and a few viruses). Some antibiotics are produced naturally, others are man-made. Some work alone, others in combination. Some are narrow-spectrum (very specific), others are broad-spectrum.

The information below is designed to give some idea of how and when antibiotics might be prescribed. The commercial or brand name is given first, followed by the generic name in brackets.

The information in no way constitutes medical advice and in no way suggests or advises the use or non-use of any medication.

When the *INFECTION* is bacterial, antibiotics might be prescribed for the following conditions:

✦ **Ear infections**: Penicillin-type drugs, such as Augmentin (amoxillin/clavulanate potassium). **Otitis media** can occur as a primary illness or as an after-effect of respiratory infections; it can be viral or bacterial. Studies have shown that a large proportion of acute ear infections (sudden onset, single episodes, known as acute otitis media) clear up on their own, without medical treatment.

✦ Sinusitis: Augmentin.

✦ 'Strep throat'/Streptococcus A infection: Pen-Vee K, Veetids (Penicillin V).

✦ Upper respiratory infections: Zithromax (azythromycin), Ceftin or Zinnet (cefuroxime exetil), Omnicef (cefdinir), Biaxin (clarithromycin), Cefzil (cefprozil).

✦ Pneumonia: Zithromax, Zinacef, Omnicef, Biaxin.

✦ Urinary tract infections, some forms of diarrhoea e.g. shigellosis: Bactrim or Septra.

✦ Skin infections e.g. impetigo: Keflex or Ketab (cephalexin), Penicillins.

When not to use antibiotics

The American Centre for Disease Control and the Academy of Paediatrics, along with several other organisations, have issued extensive guidelines, but, in summary, where the infection is not bacterial, the following applies:

✦ Sore throats: antibiotics are not usually prescribed without a positive test for Streptococcus A or other bacterial infection.

✦ Bronchitis: bronchitis or non-specific cough illnesses generally do not warrant antibiotics, although a round of antibiotics may be prescribed if the cough lasts for more than 10 days and bacteria are suspected.

✦ Colds: colds are caused by a virus, so antibiotics are not usually effective against them, but may be prescribed for bacterial infections associated with the cold.

✦ Sinus infections: these can be associated with both bacterial and viral infections, so antibiotics are not usually given unless both nasal discharge and cough persist without improvement after several days (although facial swelling, facial pain or high fever may warrant earlier treatment).

✦ Ear infections: short curative courses of antibiotics may be prescribed for single episodes of *MIDDLE EAR INFECTIONS* (acute otitis media/AOM) in healthy children older than two years, whereas preventive antibiotics might be given after three or more separate cases of AOM diagnosed over a 6–12 month period.

✦ Where there is a pre-existing condition or medication that will not interact well with antibiotics (e.g. allergy, stomach disorder), these will not be prescribed.

Possible side effects include:

✦ allergic reaction

✦ nausea

✦ drowsiness.

Further information

Straightforward medical information: www.myDr.com.au/Healthsearch/search.asp (accessed 20 September 2005)

UK Department of Health, www.dh.gov.uk (and use A–Z option) (accessed 20 September 2005)

➤➤ Anxious, shy, withdrawn children

These behaviours are often tied to **developmental stage** and age, *TEMPERAMENT AND PERSONALITY*, or to models of behaviour exhibited by those around the child (e.g. overprotective adults). The behaviours tend to fall into two categories: apathy/withdrawal and **anxiety**/fear. Girls appear to be slightly more vulnerable than boys, and children who are fearful in the preschool period are at greater risk of later depressive **disorders**.

Symptoms

Many children show some of the following behaviours at times, but when they persist and seriously affect the child's functioning and happiness, they deserve particular attention:

+ changes in *EATING BEHAVIOURS*
+ excessive worrying (e.g. about routines, what if…?)
+ fearful of people, animals, activities (in general or specific terms)
+ dependency on comfort behaviour (e.g. thumb-sucking, 'security' item)
+ often feels ill, may vomit
+ overdependence on adults
+ refusing to join in
+ sad, lacking expression
+ secondary enuresis (*BED-WETTING*)
+ *SELECTIVE MUTISM*
+ *SLEEP PROBLEMS*
+ wanders around, lack of initiative.

Causes

The causes of such behaviour may include one or more of the following:

+ family problems (e.g. arguments, financial anxieties)
+ language delay
+ maternal depression
+ *CHILD ABUSE*
+ overprotective parents (e.g. acute worry after another child has died)
+ trauma (e.g. death in the family, new baby, refugee status)
+ cultural differences and expectations.

Strategies

If possible, look for plausible explanations (e.g. is the child normally shy? what is happening at home? has the child been ill?). Where doubts and concerns persist, it is time to take further steps, which may include:

✦ Professional evaluation: (e.g. psychologist, paediatrician). Recommendations may then be made for some form of *PSYCHOTHERAPY* (e.g. play, art, family), a *BEHAVIOUR MANAGEMENT* programme or medical treatment.

✦ Behaviour management: behavioural strategies help to identify the problem/s, structure the environment/expectations, change adult models/reactions and provide positive attention for the child's increasing participation and confidence.

✦ Time and understanding: when it is established that there is no particular problem related to the child's state, allowing extra time for the child to relax, along with guided help to gradually participate, can help (e.g. taking things in small steps, preparing the child for changes of routine, a communication board for a non-verbal child, or a child without the dominant language, to indicate needs until they are able/confident to do so verbally).

✦ Cultural understanding: where children are not able to speak the dominant language of care and education settings, additional language support will be needed, as well as some means for the child to communicate needs and wants without experiencing frustration, anxiety or embarrassment. Moreover, it is important to have some understanding of what is expected and acceptable at home from a cultural standpoint.

Further information

Anxiety Attack Resource, www.anxiety-attack-web.info (accessed 20 September 2005)

www.childhoodanxietynetwork.org (accessed 20 September 2005)

➤➤ Asperger's Disorder

Asperger's refers to **significant** difficulties in social and communication skills, despite normal **intelligence** and *LANGUAGE AND SPEECH* development (although language use and understanding in social situations is a particular problem). Across the literature there still appears to be some indecision as to **'disorder'** or **'syndrome'**, but this entry refers to Asperger's Disorder. Asperger's Disorder is thought to be a neurological disorder; there appears to be a familial link and it seems to be more common in males.

Characteristics

General characteristics include:

✦ poor social skills, including communication skills (e.g. use of language, reading facial expressions)
✦ literal interpretation of explanations
✦ difficulties with change, obsessive about routines
✦ preoccupation/isolated skill with a particular subject/interest
✦ physical awkwardness
✦ hypersensitivity (e.g. to clothing, certain food, sounds).

Moreover, the person with Asperger's Disorder:

✦ perceives the world differently and 'odd' behaviours are not intentional or the result of 'bad parenting'
✦ is socially naive and frequently suffers from teasing and *BULLYING*
✦ may have coexisting difficulties (e.g. *DYSLEXIA*), causing diagnostic confusion
✦ can present with mild to severe characteristics.

Diagnosis

Asperger's Disorder tends to be recognised somewhat later than similar disorders (e.g. *AUTISM*) because many characteristic behaviours only become noticeable as the child develops; for example:

✦ language abnormalities and motor clumsiness become more apparent in the preschool period
✦ difficulties with social behaviour and obsessive interests are more noticeable when the child starts school
✦ problems with empathy, social interaction and friendships emerge towards adolescence.

Asperger's Disorder is an autism spectrum disorder or a *PERVASIVE DEVELOPMENTAL DISORDER (PDD)*. There is no single diagnostic test;

assessment includes:

✦ family and schooling background interviews to establish developmental, family and health history and school progress, along with checklists/rating scales (e.g. Gillam Asperger's Disorder Scale)

✦ direct observation of the child

✦ a thorough physical examination, including hearing and vision tests

✦ speech and language evaluation

✦ use of DSM-IV criteria or equally well-regarded criteria (e.g. Icd-10, WHO, 1992).

Treatment

This may include:

✦ behavioural intervention

✦ parent and school education

✦ individual and family counselling and therapies.

Prognosis

Asperger's Disorder is a lifelong disorder, but early diagnosis and intervention can minimise its effects. Children with Asperger's Disorder are usually quite capable academically and can participate in regular learning settings. However, special education services may be needed to help with a coexisting difficulty (e.g. Dyslexia), with learning difficulties related to the nature of Asperger's itself (e.g. language usage, obsessive interests) and/or to help carers and teachers understand the Asperger's child.

Language usage and literal interpretation of information can often cause problems, both in terms of social and school learning success. Children with Asperger's Disorder are puzzled by, or sometimes unaware of, their failure to 'connect'. They often pick up on information that is not highly relevant, or will misinterpret it. Their analysis of an issue can be unusual and, while quite interesting, it may be inappropriate to class teaching and learning goals. These kinds of problems can lead to school failure, frustration, sadness and low **self-esteem**.

Sometimes the person with Asperger's Disorder may also fall back on patterns of unusual behaviour out of **anxiety** or insecurity, and may experience *DEPRESSION*.

Further information

O.A.S.I.S. Online Asperger Syndrome Information and Support, www.udel.edu/bkirby/asperger (accessed 20 September 2005)

www.tonyattwood.com.au (accessed 20 September 2005)

➤➤ Asthma

Asthma is a chronic inflammatory disorder of the airways characterised by recurrent episodes of wheezing, breathlessness, chest tightness and coughing. Asthma can begin at any age and there is evidence that Asthma among children is increasing.

Causes

The exact cause is not known, but a number of factors have been identified (e.g. muscle disease, fluid build-up/oedema, cell malfunction), and several factors are known to increase the risk of developing Asthma:

✦ family history

✦ smoking during pregnancy

✦ irritants in the work environment

✦ environmental pollution.

When a person with Asthma comes into contact with an irritant, the muscles of the airways tighten, the airways swell, mucus (phlegm) is produced and this causes further **inflammation**, leading to the symptoms of Asthma. Irritants vary from person to person, but include colds, smoke, exercise and *ALLERGIES*.

Symptoms

These include:

✦ wheezing/whistling noise in the chest

✦ shortness of breath

✦ coughing

✦ feeling of tightness in the chest.

Diagnosis

In children under about seven or eight years of age, diagnosis is based mainly on a history of wheezing that cannot be explained by anything else (e.g. a cold, heart problems), because young children in particular are not able to reliably perform a lung function test. A health and family history is also gathered, because close relatives with Asthma and the presence of some other allergic conditions (e.g. *ECZEMA*, hives) can support the diagnosis.

Treatment

This can be as straightforward as avoiding Asthma 'triggers', or it may be medication, via an inhaler or tablets. Inhalers are small, hand-held devices that, when pumped, spray the medication directly into the mouth and thus into the airways. They come in various forms:

✦ Relievers (bronchodilator inhaler, usually blue applicator), used three to four times per week, act to relax the muscles of narrowed airways.

✦ Preventers (anti-inflammatory inhaler, usually brown, red or orange applicator), used every day for a period of time, to allow the medication to build up, controlling swelling.

✦ Symptom controllers (long-acting medication) that can be added to the inhaler.

Children should have a personal Asthma medication card and action plan, and child care and education staff should be advised of correct action, but the principles are:

✦ Use the reliever inhaler, sit up, loosen clothing.

✦ If there is no relief, the child should continue to take a puff every minute and emergency medical advice/help should be sought.

Prognosis

Poorly controlled Asthma can limit or prevent participation in many social and physical activities, but with early diagnosis and proper treatment, most people with Asthma can lead perfectly normal lives.

Further information

AsthmaUK, www.asthma.org.uk (accessed 20 September 2005)

Australian Asthma website, www.nationalasthma.org.au (accessed 20 September 2005)

▶▶ Attention Deficit Disorders (ADD): An overview

Most people at times have difficulty sitting still or paying attention because they are bored or distracted, but this is only temporary. For people with ADD, the problem is so persistent that it interferes with daily life at home, at school, at work and socially. Consistently poor attention and concentration is also often accompanied by excessive impulsivity (doing things without thinking first), and/or Hyperactivity (endless fiddling, physical movement). ADD are thought to affect between 3 and 5 per cent of school-age children.

ADD may also be referred to as Attention Deficit/Hyperactivity **Disorder** (AD/HD); but take special notice of the backslash, which underlines the fact that someone can have an attention deficit disorder that does not necessarily include Hyperactivity.

Causes

- ✦ Neuro-biological: nerve cells and pathways carry messages to and from the brain, determining our actions and responses to incoming information from the world around us. In the case of ADD it appears that there is an underproduction of substances that regulate these brain messages.
- ✦ **Genetics**: children with ADD often have a family history of similar problems (e.g. a parent or grandparent had trouble at school with behaviour and/or learning). Studies show that the likelihood of ADD increases by about 30 per cent if there is a sibling with an ADD, and by about 50 per cent if there is a parent with an ADD.
- ✦ Diet and food *ALLERGIES* are not thought to be primary causes. There are some foods that can trigger unusual activity (and inactivity) levels and inattentive behaviours, and these appear to aggravate ADD behaviours, without being the cause of an ADD itself.
- ✦ Bad parenting does not cause ADD, although, again, it is thought that certain family life factors (e.g. overanxious parents, disorganised routines) can aggravate some ADD behaviours.

Diagnosis

There is no single diagnostic test and a comprehensive evaluation is necessary. DSM-IV criteria are the most common standard applied and various professionals with appropriate experience and knowledge can reliably diagnose ADD (e.g. *EDUCATIONAL PSYCHOLOGISTS*, **neurologists**, medical doctors).

Evaluation should include:

◆ assessment of academic, social and emotional functioning and **developmental stage**

◆ a careful history from parents, teachers and, where appropriate, the child

◆ checklists for rating ADD symptoms and ruling out other disabilities

◆ medical assessments (thorough physical examination, hearing/vision tests, thyroid functioning).

Prognosis

Children with ADD are usually of normal **intelligence**, but they sometimes struggle to realise their potential. In addition, ADD can cause a developmental delay of two to four years, making children seem less mature than their peers.

Poor concentration and frequent criticism of behaviour can lead to low **self-esteem**, underachievement and *DEPRESSION*.

Adolescents with ADD present a special challenge. Academic and organisational demands increase and typical adolescent issues present themselves (e.g. establishing independence, peer pressure, exposure to alcohol and other drugs, emerging sexuality).

The earlier the diagnosis and intervention, the better the prognosis.

Further information

ADDNetUK, www.btinternet.com/~black.ice (accessed 20 September 2005)

Parent Magic, Inc., parenting solutions, www.parentmagic.com (accessed 20 September 2005)

➤➤ Attention Deficit Disorders: DSM-IV criteria

The **Diagnostic and Statistical Manual (DSM-IV**, recently revised) is a publication of the American Psychiatric Association.

It has been paraphrased and presented here to make the diagnosis and characteristics of ADD quite clear, and to dispel some of the misunderstandings and myths that surround the **disorder**. The DSM-IV entry for ADD identifies three categories of ADD:

✦ predominately inattentive
✦ predominately hyperactive-impulsive
✦ combined.

A person must satisfy the following criteria (NB child-specific examples only are listed here):

A Either (1) OR (2)

1 Six (or more) of the following symptoms of inattention have persisted for at least six months at a level that is **maladaptive** and inconsistent with developmental level.

Inattention. Often:

a fails to give close attention to details, makes careless mistakes in schoolwork/other activities
b has difficulty sustaining attention in tasks, play activities
c does not seem to listen when spoken to directly
d does not seem to follow through on instructions, fails to finish schoolwork, chores (not due to defiance/naughtiness or failure to understand instructions)
e has difficulty organising tasks, activities
f avoids, dislikes or is reluctant to do tasks requiring sustained mental effort (e.g. homework)
g loses things (e.g. toys, pencils, books)
h is distracted by unimportant information
i is forgetful in daily activities.

2 Six, or more, of the following symptoms of hyperactivity-impulsivity have persisted for at least six months at a level that is maladaptive and inconsistent with developmental stage.

Hyperactivity. Often:

a fidgets with hands or feet, squirms in seat
b is out of seat where it is inappropriate

c   runs about or climbs excessively where it is inappropriate

d   has difficulty playing quietly

e   is 'on the go', acts as if 'driven by a motor'

f   talks excessively.

Impulsivity. Often:

g   blurts out answer before question is completed

h   has difficulty waiting turns

i   interrupts/intrudes on others (e.g. conversations, games).

B   Some hyperactive-impulsive or inattentive symptoms present before the age of seven years.

C   Some interference from the symptoms is evident in two or more settings (e.g. school and home).

D   There must be clear evidence of **significant** interference in social and academic functioning.

E   The symptoms are not better accounted for by another disorder (e.g. learning disorder, personality disorder).

Further information

Online psychological services, www.psychologynet.org (accessed 20 September 2005)

►► Attention Deficit Disorders: Management

Management should take a multidisciplinary approach and can include:

✦ an appropriate educational programme
✦ *BEHAVIOUR MANAGEMENT* strategies
✦ individual and family counselling and parent training
✦ medication, when required
✦ *NATUROPATHY.*

Appropriate education programme

Children with ADD can usually be taught in a regular classroom, sometimes with adjustments to the environment (e.g. reducing background noise) and behaviour management. Some children require learning support to help negate the effects of poor concentration.

Behaviour management

Behaviour management operates on the principle that behaviours can be increased or decreased according to the consequences that the child receives for those behaviours. Strategies include setting clear rules and guidelines, being consistent in expectations and using reinforcement to encourage/discourage behaviour (e.g. special privileges, withdrawal of privileges).

Individual and family counselling and parent training

PSYCHOTHERAPY can help with mood swings, social difficulties and discouragement. Help with problem-solving, communication and **self-advocacy** skills may also be needed.

Parents can be helped to understand ADD, can be taught behaviour management strategies and can be encouraged to seek appropriate counselling for themselves and the child.

Medication

Medication is not needed by all children with ADD and it should not be prescribed automatically. However, medication such as Ritalin can improve attention and concentration, compliance, effort on tasks, and amount and accuracy of schoolwork produced; and it can decrease activity levels, impulsivity, negative behaviours in social interactions and physical and verbal hostility.

Children on medication should be monitored closely by their physician, parents and carers.

Naturopathy

There has been considerable research into the benefits of naturopathic remedies and supplements, among them products such as Efalex, evening primrose oil and the Omega oils. The basic premise is that fatty acids oils are essential for efficient brain cell functioning and that supplementing these oils can have a positive effect on such functioning.

Scientific research and conclusions are not extensive as yet, and personal/anecdotal reports from parents indicate mixed results.

Prognosis

Without treatment, people with ADD can experience social and academic failure, career underachievement, low **self-esteem** and an increased risk of antisocial behaviour. However, studies show that early identification and adequate treatment lead to fewer problems with school, peers and substance abuse, and show improved overall functioning. In adulthood, roughly one-third of people with ADD lead fairly normal lives; about half have symptoms that can interfere with social relationships or job performance; and severe problems persist in about 10 per cent of adults.

Further information

ADDNetUK, www.btinternet.com/~black.ice (accessed 20 September 2005)
ADDers, www.adders.org (accessed 20 September 2005)

➤➤ Attention Deficit Disorders: Medication

Anyone about to take medication should have:

+ a documented assessment by a qualified practitioner

+ a physical examination (medical history, blood pressure, weight, *ALLERGIES*, **EEG**, blood analysis); the record should indicate other regular medication (e.g. Tegratol for *EPILEPSY*)

+ a family history taken that describes health and psychological/psychiatric problems, including drug or alcohol abuse.

A 'milligram × body weight' formula is usually used to calculate initial dosage. It should be trialled for a set period (e.g. one week) and the child observed for positive and negative effects. The prescribing specialist should be visited weekly until a medication level is established.

The person taking/administering the medication should know:

+ the purpose, dosage and possible side effects

+ what action to take for disturbing side effects or if the medication fails to have a positive effect

+ capsules should not be broken open

+ no tablets or capsules should be chewed

+ to take medication with water only (not milk, juices, soft drinks).

Medication is not a cure-all. Research shows that a combination of medication and *BEHAVIOUR MANAGEMENT* is the most effective treatment for ADD.

The prescribing specialist should always be consulted before discontinuing medication, as a sudden decrease in medication can cause unwanted side effects.

Stimulants

+ Stimulants such as Ritalin and Methylin (methylphenidate) are fast-release tablets, which produce results in 15–20 minutes, the effects of which last for 3–4 hours.

+ Slow- or extended-release forms (often shown as SR or ER) can have an effect for 6–8 hours, and there is less need to remember/be reminded to take medication (minimising the embarrassment that some children feel about taking medicines at school).

+ Concerta is a methylphenidate, but effects can last 10–12 hours.

✦ Mixed amphetamines such as Adderall generally have longer-lasting effects and are thought to have a gentler side-effects 'profile'. They come in fast- and slow-release forms.

✦ Dexedrine and Dextrostat (dextroamphetamine) are twice as powerful as Ritalin (and dosages are calculated accordingly). They are available as tablets or capsules. Dexedrine Spansules (capsules) are slow-release.

Antidepressants

Antidepressants, such as Tofranil, Norpramin, Pamelor, Buproprion/ Wellbutrin, may take 1–3 weeks for the full effects to be felt, but usually last for 24 hours.

Anti-hypertensives

Considered for very hyperactive children with low frustration tolerance and for reducing tics and sleeplessness. Catapres (clonadine), which is also available in patches, and Tenex fall under this category.

Side effects

Carers of children on ADD medication should look for unusual appetite loss, sleeplessness, headaches, nervousness, irritability, excessive crying, sadness, staring into space.

Further information

ADDNetUK, www.btinternet.com/~black.ice (accessed 20 September 2005)

ADDers, www.adders.org (accessed 20 September 2005)

Parent Magic, Inc., parenting solutions, www.parentmagic.com (accessed 20 September 2005)

➤➤ Autism

Autism is a neurobiological **disorder** that can vary greatly in severity. It is often referred to as Autistic Spectrum Disorder and is also considered a *PERVASIVE DEVELOPMENTAL DISORDER.*

Autism affects an estimated 4 or 5 people out of every 10,000, and the ratio of males to females is 4:1. The 'frigid parent' **syndrome** (where the disorder was blamed on emotionally 'cold' and unresponsive parents, particularly the mother) has long been disproved.

Symptoms of Autism appear between birth and three years. People with Autism have a normal life expectancy, but Autism is a lifelong disorder.

Characteristics (varying severity)

Social interaction

+ rejects/is uninterested in physical contact
+ poor social skills (e.g. language, eye contact)
+ isolated, withdrawn, unaware of others
+ interrupts/cannot be interrupted.

Verbal/non-verbal communication

+ language may be delayed/not develop at all
+ voice abnormalities (e.g. expressionless, too loud)
+ trouble with various aspects of language (e.g. meaning, personal pronouns)
+ language anomalies (e.g. echolalia – repeating the language of others).

Activities and interests

+ obsessive interest/s and/or manipulation of objects
+ minimal/no play skills
+ repetitive movements (e.g. rocking, hand flicking)
+ intolerant of change
+ over/under-sensitive to noises, textures, etc.

Causes

Research indicates:
+ **genetic** links
+ environmental factors (e.g. viruses, chemicals)
+ foetal brain abnormalities
+ brain molecule abnormalities.

Diagnosis

A **multidisciplinary team** (e.g. medical doctor, *EDUCATIONAL PSYCHOLOGIST*, *SPEECH AND LANGUAGE THERAPIST*) uses various tools, including diagnostic criteria (e.g. DSM-IV/IV-R) and rating scales (e.g. Childhood Autism Rating Scale /CARS). A family and developmental history is taken, observations and interactive sessions establish *SOCIAL-EMOTIONAL DEVELOPMENT*, *LANGUAGE AND SPEECH*, motor and cognitive skills, and a thorough physical examination, including hearing and vision, rules out medical causes.

Autism can coexist with other difficulties (e.g. *EPILEPSY*) and can also be confused with other disorders (e.g. Childhood Schizophrenia, *ASPERGER'S DISORDER*).

Prognosis

The majority of people with Autism score in the low to below-average range on **IQ tests**, but language and behaviour difficulties can make *TESTING* unreliable. A small percentage of people have highly specialised but often limited or impractical skills (e.g. can understand Calculus, but cannot work out change at the shop).

With early intervention, mildly autistic children can often cope in mainstream care and education settings, although particular understanding and support is usually needed.

Treatment

A combination of strategies is often prescribed, including:

✦ *BEHAVIOUR MANAGEMENT*/education: highly structured, intensive training that focuses on social and language skills (e.g. **applied behaviour analysis (ABA)**)

✦ medication: drugs can reduce self-injurious or aggressive behaviour, as well as treat associated conditions (e.g. epilepsy)

✦ therapeutic intervention: some forms of *PSYCHOTHERAPY* (e.g. art, music, movement) can ease the severity of some behaviours (e.g. distress, aggression), and can help parents, siblings and other family members understand and cope with the disorder.

Further information

Association for Autistically Handicapped/AUTISM Independent UK, www.autismuk.com (accessed 20 September 2005)

National Autistic Society, www.nas.org.uk (accessed 20 September 2005)

►► Bed-wetting (enuresis)

Bed-wetting usually decreases with age (about 10 per cent of 6-year-olds compared to 3 per cent of 14-year-olds wet the bed), and boys tend to toilet-train and stay dry slightly later than girls. It is considered to be problematic in children over about 6 years of age.

Problematic bed-wetting is considered to be either Primary (if the child has never been dry, or only occasionally dry, at night), or Secondary (bed-wetting after a child has been dry at night for a considerable length of time). Primary enuresis is more common.

In either case, the child should have a thorough medical check-up, in case there is a medical condition causing the problem. If a physical **disorder** is not diagnosed, then advice and support can be sought from various professionals (e.g. psychologist, psychotherapist).

Primary functional enuresis (chronic bed-wetting)

Causes

Possible causes include:

+ physically and/or neurologically immature bladder
+ underproduction of Vasopressin, the antidiuretic hormone which controls the production of urine
+ deep sleeping pattern (so deeply asleep that they are not aware of the message the bladder sends to the brain saying it is full)
+ an inherited condition (someone else in the family has/had the same problem)
+ increased tendency in children with *ATTENTION DEFICIT DISORDER*, learning difficulties or *ALLERGIES*.

Effects

Any of the following may result:

+ embarrassment, by about age 6; child will not go on overnight school trips, to a friend's house to sleep, etc.
+ low **self-image**, may be teased by siblings, peers
+ parents may feel they have failed as 'parents'
+ parents may also get angry, feel frustrated or anxious, and communicate this to the child.

Treatment (always seek professional advice)

✦ Time – many children outgrow the condition.

As children mature, their muscles become stronger, their bladder capacity increases and they tend to sleep less deeply, increasing their awareness of the messages the bladder sends to the brain. However, time may not be an option if the child is at risk of social and emotional unhappiness.

✦ Medical – treatment usually consists of one of two drugs.

Imipramine (Tofranil) is thought to either improve sleeping behaviour or the functioning of the smooth muscles of the bladder. Symptoms often return when the medication is discontinued, however, and it can have serious side effects.

Desmopressin Acetate is a synthetic anti-diuretic hormone designed to decrease urine production, thus reducing the chances that the bladder will overfill during sleep. It is administered as a nasal spray. The medication often works quickly, but symptoms may return when it is discontinued. This medication is considered safer than Tofranil, but can still have side effects.

✦ Behavioural – may be used alone or in combination with medication.

While this may take somewhat longer to have an effect, improvement is usually maintained. Several methods can be used:

a   Retention control training can increase the capacity of the bladder and strengthen the muscle that holds back urination. The child is taught to control urinating during the day by postponing it, initially for a minute or two, and then for gradually increasing amounts of time.

b   Night-lifting involves waking the child periodically during the night to go to the bathroom. The child walks independently to the bathroom, urinates and then goes back to bed, thus learning to wake and go to the bathroom during the night to empty the bladder, and so stay dry.

c   Moisture alarms can be a successful way to treat bed-wetting. The alarm is a sensor, clipped to the bed-clothing, that sounds when the child begins to wet the bed. The child wakes, goes to the bathroom to finish urinating, then goes back to bed and to sleep. This pattern slowly conditions the brain to respond appropriately, during sleep, to messages from the bladder.

d   Hypnosis uses repeated listening to a hypnosis tape to reprogramme the brain to respond to full bladder messages while the child is asleep, in the same way s/he responds when awake.

Secondary enuresis

Causes

✦ Stresses in a child's life. The three most common triggers are: hospitalisation, starting school and the birth of a sibling.

Other stress factors include tense or argumentative family relationships, a death in the family, *CHILD ABUSE* or an **anxiety** disorder.

✦ Physical/medical problems.

Effects

The effects on the child and family are similar to those described for primary enuresis. However, in addition to the stress caused by bed-wetting, there will be the trigger events themselves to deal with, and/or the worry over a medical condition.

Treatment

✦ Medical

Medical assessment and advice should always be sought in the first instance, either to eliminate the possibility of a medical condition or to have it diagnosed and proper treatment begun.

✦ Behavioural

BEHAVIOUR MANAGEMENT strategies can help to identify the cause of the problem and bring about changes to the setting, to adult reactions and to the child.

✦ Psychotherapy

Various types of *PSYCHOTHERAPY* (e.g. play therapy, art therapy, family therapy) can provide stress-free environments for the child and/or the family, to help them resolve the individual or group factors that have triggered Secondary enuresis.

Further information

Enuresis Research and Information Centre, www.enuresis.org.uk (accessed 20 September 2005)

➤➤ Behaviour Management: Principles

Behaviour Management strategies are based on the early theories of scientists such as Pavlov and Skinner. These largely laboratory-based theories have since been developed, refined and modified into a practical approach to improving behaviour.

Basic principles

✦ If a behaviour gets us what we want, we tend to repeat it; and if that pattern of 'behaviour and response' happens often enough, then we keep the behaviour, be it good or bad.

✦ To stop a behaviour we must receive a response to it that makes us doubt its usefulness. We then try first to 'fix' the behaviour (e.g. do it more extremely). If this does not work, we look for alternatives.

✦ If the response to the alternative is pleasant and consistent we reject the 'old' behaviour.

Terminology

✦ Appropriate/inappropriate behaviours are the behaviours you want to start or stop. (Avoid words such as good or bad – they can be confusing.)

✦ Reinforcement (motivators) can be positive (anything that increases the chances of starting or stopping a behaviour) or negative (the opposite; for example, giving a child a sweet to stop a tantrum may increase the chances of another tantrum). Avoid negatives at all costs.

✦ Rewards are reinforcements given only for appropriate behaviour. They can be primary (e.g. a sweet, a gold star) or secondary (e.g. verbal praise, a smile).

✦ Punishments are also reinforcements, but only given for inappropriate behaviour. They too can be primary (e.g. time out, removal of toys/games) or secondary (e.g. withdrawing attention). Punishment does NOT include smacking or any other physical act towards the child. Apart from the fact that physical punishment (e.g. smacking) might be illegal (depending on what country you live in), it has not been found to be an effective behaviour management strategy.

Remember:

✦ Expectations must be realistic.

✦ Responses to behaviours must be clear and consistent. If the response pattern is broken, the value of the new behaviour is put in doubt.

✦ Behaviour management is not just about inappropriate behaviour. Actively look for and reward appropriate behaviours.

✦ Anger or excessive talking should not be used in response to inappropriate behaviour. This focuses attention on that behaviour and is negative reinforcement.

✦ Choose motivators carefully, because one child's reward can be another's punishment. Motivators must be practical (no exaggerated 'threats' or 'rewards'); at first they need to be highly visible and instantaneous.

✦ Progress from regular, frequent primary rewards to secondary rewards, until the 'well-being' that comes from being 'good' is enough in itself.

✦ Inappropriate behaviour tends to get more extreme before being rejected altogether and there may be anger and upset as the child learns to exchange what was 'comfortable' for what is new and initially less comfortable.

✦ A behaviour management programme must be well planned and reviewed weekly.

Further information

www.learningandteaching.info/learning/behaviour-mod.htm (accessed 20 September 2005)

➤➤ Behaviour Management: The practice

The most important reason for changing behaviour must be to help the child be a happier person. A side benefit will be to make adults' lives happier; but do it for the child first and foremost.

Basic steps

This is not a prescription for 'do-it-yourself', but an overview of the steps usually taken.

✦ Define the inappropriate behaviours (what they are, when they happen, how others respond and what effect it has on the child).

✦ Gather information and advice (e.g. from parents, teachers) before adopting a particular course of action. Sometimes the child is ill, there may have been a family trauma, the child may have a learning difficulty, and so on, and behaviour management may not be suitable/necessary.

✦ If there are particular situations (e.g. time of day, place) that set off the behaviour, or make it worse, then try doing something about them first, or as well, rather than focusing solely on the child. It may save a lot of time.

✦ If behaviour management is the most suitable strategy, the next step is deciding what behaviours would be more appropriate than those causing the problem.

✦ Decide what is likely to encourage the child to behave or not behave a certain way (i.e. rewards and punishment).

✦ Explain the 'rules' to the child, making sure s/he understands why something will/will not happen, and also giving him/her an opportunity to change of his/her free will. (It is not unusual for children to get the message just from this discussion and to modify the behaviour/s themselves without much more intervention, particularly when they already know that their behaviour is over the top.)

✦ Avoid long explanations and DO NOT debate the 'rules'. If they are fair and positive then no further explanations are needed.

✦ Keep language simple and consistent (e.g. 'No, if you can't play nicely, you can't play at all. When you're ready to play nicely, come and tell me.').

✦ Actively look for chances to positively reinforce. Do not react only when the child behaves inappropriately.

✦ Avoid ultimatums from which the child or you cannot 'escape' without embarrassment or confrontation.

✦ If you feel yourself getting angry, walk away or ask someone else to take over.

◆ Keep records (e.g. a simple checklist/tally sheet) to help judge objectively the success/failure of a strategy.

◆ Expect the behaviour to become worse before it gets better, and be particularly careful to maintain the programme quite firmly during that phase.

◆ Review progress weekly. Avoid changing the programme unless something is proving impractical or ineffective, or a response is found to be particularly effective.

➤➤ Bilingualism/multilingualism:

Terminology

Bilingualism is the use of two languages to communicate; multilingualism refers to the use of more than two languages. This entry will refer to bilingualism because it is the more common situation; English will be used as the model for the first language – solely because English is the cultural language of this book and this writer.

Bilingualism can mean different things to different people (e.g. levels of fluency). Moreover, keywords are used in different ways by different people whenever bilingualism is being discussed, and it is important to define them.

✦ Home language is the language most often used in the home.

✦ First language/mother tongue is the language the child speaks most fluently (and is not always the home language).

✦ Majority/dominant language is the language of the wider community or country where the child lives.

✦ Bilingual learner refers to a person learning formal skills (e.g. school subjects) in a language other than their first language.

✦ Bilingual education is the use of two languages for instruction.

✦ Bilingual setting is a setting (e.g. a school) where there are users of two different languages.

Types of bilingualism

✦ Equal ability: the ability to speak two languages with equal proficiency/ skill/fluency in the various aspects of language (speaking, writing, etc.).

✦ One language dominant: one language is more proficient, in all or most aspects.

✦ Semi-lingualism: sometimes used to describe poor proficiency in both languages (relative to someone who is monolingual).

Approaches to developing bilingualism

✦ Balanced: two languages are learned simultaneously (realistically only an option for children who have not already acquired a first language).

✦ Sequential/successive: for children who have an established first language before learning a second language.

➤➤ Bilingualism: Acquisition

Children are believed to acquire two languages either by simultaneous language learning or as a successive or sequential language.

Balanced/simultaneous bilingualism

+ One parent, one language; for example, if mother is English mother-tongue and father is Italian mother-tongue, then mum speaks English to the child, and dad speaks Italian, even if the parents speak English and/or Italian between themselves.
+ One language at home, one at school (e.g. Singhalese at home, English at school).
+ One language at home and school, one in the community (e.g. English at home and school, Spanish in the community).
+ Both parents speak both languages to the child, but set activities and/or times are scheduled; for example, English is spoken after school and for bedtime stories; Swedish is spoken at the dinner table; or maybe it is Swedish and English on alternate days.
+ Consistency is vital. If the child hears mixed models and conversations there is a risk that this is the type of language that will develop. Mixing up words and syntax is common when learning any language (first or otherwise), but it is tied to **developmental stages**; outside of those stages it can be problematic.
+ Both languages should be considered equally important.
+ If the child is exposed to one language far more than the other (e.g. one language dominates at school and in the community, and the other language only occurs at home), then ensure balance through additional, quality exposure to the less used and heard language (e.g. videos, books).

Sequential acquisition

+ The speed of acquisition and level of proficiency depends on the individual (age, developmental stage, **aptitude**, community/family attitudes, exposure, first-language proficiency, etc.).
+ Learners learn how to use their additional language in much the same way as they did their first; for example, by generalising a rule (e.g. putting '-ed' on the end of all past tense verbs, before learning about the exceptions of irregular verbs, such as 'begin/began').
+ Learners start learning their second language at different ages and thus use different learning strategies (according to developmental age/stage).

✦ Acquisition proceeds in a fairly common sequence regardless of languages and settings.

✦ Some aspects of the second language are learned when the learner has a need to know them.

✦ Some items can be learned in no particular sequence.

✦ There may be factors that do not allow the early learning of certain items (e.g. 4-year-olds may struggle to use plurals because developmentally they are not able to do so accurately, even in their first language).

✦ There is a difference between the language learning of younger and older children; for example, younger children might acquire a more 'unaccented' pronunciation, but older learners have more learning strategies that help them learn more quickly; younger learners are learning language and developmental concepts alongside each other, while older children learn new labels for concepts that are already familiar.

✦ Learners and their learning strategies change over time.

✦ 'Inter-language' is the term sometimes used to describe the language that learners produce as they progress. It changes as the learner learns more, and it is thought by some researchers and practitioners that noting linguistic errors could be used to assess where a child is at in the second-language learning process.

✦ Continued support of the first language helps second-language learners.

✦ **Decoding** skills (e.g. letter/sound matching, phonic rules) and exposure to reading materials are needed for the second language learner to develop reading skills and comprehension.

✦ Language learning activities need to be well structured and planned for all ages and stages of development and learning. Statements like 'all children can learn a second language when they are young' are oversimplifications.

How long does it take?

Most discussions make a difference between:

✦ conversational fluency (to socialise/communicate with peers, etc.), and

✦ academic language proficiency (able to learn school curriculum material successfully in the second language, and a goal of bilingual education).

Conversational fluency is thought to take 1–2 years of exposure to the second language, while academic grade-appropriate proficiency, comparable to monolingual English speakers, takes at least 5 years.

Learning activities

These need to be appropriate to age and learning stage; for example:

✦ For new learners and younger learners, provide practical activities and tasks (simple naming, word/picture matching), supported by obvious contextual clues (e.g. pictures, signs) that do not require strong academic language skills.

✦ Students who are more advanced in their language skills also need context-supported activities, but will be able to cope with more demanding, analytical tasks.

In addition, it is necessary to teach the mechanics (e.g. phonics) of skills such as reading and spelling, for speed and fluency of recognition and writing. However, it must not be assumed that these skills equal understanding, and therefore comprehension must also be taught (through exposure to vocabulary, written material, video, film, plays, etc.).

Further information

Educational ideas and solutions, www.iteachilearn.com (accessed 20 September 2005)
National Association for Language Development in the Curriculum, www.naldic.org.uk (accessed 20 September 2005)

➤➤ Bilingualism: Bilingual education

Bilingual education refers to programmes (e.g. school) that use two languages for teaching, generally for two purposes:

✦ acquisition of a second language for academic success; and/or

✦ maintenance of the first language.

Terminology

✦ EAL (English as an additional language) and ESL (English as a second language): teaching/learning of English in addition to the learner's first language. EAL recognises that for some children English may be their third or fourth language. EAL/ESL teaching and learning usually take place in mainstream settings rather than in designated language schools, with the aim of supporting language learning alongside academic/school learning, and vice versa.

✦ EFL (English as a foreign language): teaching English as a foreign language in a non-English-speaking country (e.g. teaching English in Italy).

✦ ESOL (English for speakers of other languages): teaching English to adult speakers of other languages.

Approaches

✦ Immersion programmes teach in an added/second language, although the teacher knows and can use the child's first language (e.g. teaching in English to French-speaking children, with the teacher proficient in French). The child's first language is used to speed up the learning of the second language and thus access to the school curriculum and academic success.

✦ Submersion programmes teach using the majority language, with little or no first-language support (e.g. teaching Arabic-speaking children in English with little or no use of Arabic language/s to help the children understand what is being said and/or taught).

✦ Maintenance programmes teach children in both their first language and the majority language, in order to maintain the use of the first language and culture. This approach is often used in transitional programmes where learners gradually move towards the use of the majority language for schooling.

✦ British/American international schools are not so much an approach, but a particular setting, because English is the language of instruction but is not the community language. There are significant numbers of English first-language students with no need of EAL support, students with first languages other than English (e.g. children of diplomatic families from various countries) and students from the community language (e.g. Italian first-language students at a British international school in Italy). English may be taught in various combinations; for example, English-speaking classroom teachers with varying proficiency in the child's first language; timetabled EAL curriculum teaching; and EFL lessons focusing on English language. First-language maintenance might be included in the curriculum, particularly if it is the community language or if it is a subject in the school's foreign languages programme (e.g. in the Italian example above, Japanese students probably will not study Japanese language, unless it is a school subject).

✦ Research suggests that dual-language education programmes represent the most effective way of promoting second-language acquisition.

➤➤ Birth order

There is no evidence that behaviours often associated with the first born, youngest or middle child are preprogrammed. Nor does birth order determine **intelligence** or personality. What happens sometimes, however, is that behaviours occur as a result of position in the family interacting with environment, *TEMPERAMENT AND PERSONALITY.*

For example, a younger child with an even temperament in a calm family environment might interact with an older sibling quite differently to a child at the other end of the energy-level continuum and/or in a more volatile environment. Gender too can sometimes make a difference, as can male/female order. For example, the middle of 3 girls, with a fourth sibling who is male, may feel the 'middle' child anyway.

However, studies have identified some birth order characteristics that can apply, but beware of stereotypes, myths and conclusions that do not take other factors into account.

Only child
The only child may:
+ feel incompetent because adult models can always do things better
+ be indulged, self-centred, not good at sharing or turn-taking
+ relate better to adults than to peers
+ be reliant on others
+ be self-absorbed, play alone for long periods of time.

First child
The first child may:
+ believe s/he must get and hang on to a position of superiority (may do this by being very good or misbehaving, or annoying younger sibling)
+ feel like an 'only child' until the arrival of a second child, and may resent a newborn sibling
+ be treated more, or less, leniently due to parents' inexperience with children
+ become very responsible, or lose interest in pleasing others
+ feel more pressured than the next born (e.g. to be 'grown-up', good, do well at school)
+ show some difficult or out-of-character behaviours after the novelty of a new baby has worn off and the child realises that the changes are permanent
+ need to be 'right'.

Second child

The second child may:

+ act like everything is a race or a competition, because s/he is always second to do things
+ gang up with older sibling against a new arrival, or may identify with new sibling
+ act in opposite ways to the elder child to establish own identity, to have own 'status'
+ enjoy being the 'baby' and having others do things for him/her
+ feel pressured to be like the elder sibling
+ feel very resentful when a third child arrives
+ find parents less strict or expectations less demanding, since the elder sibling has 'paved the way' and parents are less anxious
+ get angry about always being the 'baby' (e.g. 'Why can't I do it too! He always gets to do it and I never do!').

Middle child of three

The middle child of three may:

+ be more adaptable than the other two if s/he becomes used to being 'sandwiched'
+ become the 'problem' child to attract attention, to establish own position and identity
+ not have sense of who s/he is in family (i.e. not the oldest, not the youngest) and feel uncertain of importance to parents
+ resent older and/or younger siblings, and continually fight with the older and put down the younger.

Youngest child

The youngest child may:

+ expect others to do things for him/her
+ become the 'tyrant' of the family
+ behave like an only child
+ feel weak, small, that others do not take him/her seriously
+ often side with the oldest against the middle child.

Beyond the home

Children's feelings about their position and value in the family can spill over into early years and school settings. They arrive with a set of perceptions about how to get their own way, where the 'competition' is, how one deals with it, and so on.

They may also use school academic performance and behaviour to attract attention, according to their temperament, personality, academic **ability** and the success of the sibling who has gone before them.

Teachers need to take family dynamics into consideration when problem behaviours present themselves; talking with parents or with a child psychologist can provide insight into what is going on, and parents can be helped to adjust family expectations, routines and interactions.

For example:
+ Where a child feels undervalued in the family, give him/her some special status.
+ Bedtime hours can be different according to age in the family (e.g. the firstborn could be allowed a slightly later bedtime than younger siblings).
+ Pocket money can be earned by all the children, but meted out according to age (and responsibility). Older siblings earn more, but have to do more.
+ For the older sibling who is trying to establish a more grown-up identity, provide some special responsibility and status (e.g. 'Now that you are 8, you can help me tidy your room, but you can also choose your own T-shirts/your pocket money will go up by.../bedtime will be 10 minutes later').
+ Explain clearly to all the children that each one has their own age, importance, job to do, and so on, and that no one will be asked to do more than they are old enough to cope with. Just having the age/birth order issue acknowledged can often help to put it into perspective.
+ One approach to help middle children is to point out that in a way they have the best of both worlds. They are both bigger and smaller and get to do things that go with both positions.

➤➤ Bullying

Bullying is a persistent, deliberate desire to hurt another person and to put that person under stress.

✦ It can take place almost anywhere and from a young age.

✦ It is aggressive and associated with other antisocial behaviour (e.g. vandalism).

✦ Fear is always associated with bullying.

✦ If it is not openly condemned, then it may be seen as acceptable.

✦ It affects children who witness it, as well as the actual victim.

✦ Adults often underestimate/deny it (victims are 'telltales', it doesn't happen in 'my' classroom, it's just 'horseplay', etc.).

✦ If 'teasing' has malicious intent, then it is bullying.

Surveys conservatively suggest that about 9 per cent of a school population are victims and about 6 per cent are bullies.

Types of bullying

✦ Gesture: secretive, takes place where more open bullying is not possible (e.g. in the classroom).

✦ Verbal: most often related to physical appearance, race, learning difficulties.

✦ Physical: the most visible form of bullying; it is sometimes excused (e.g. 'boys will be boys'); it is not restricted to boys or to a particular age.

✦ Extortion: various forms of bullying are used to extort belongings (e.g. sweets, money, toys, mobile phones).

✦ Exclusion: underhand and subtle; often used by teenage girls.

Management strategies

✦ Reactive: action taken after the bullying is identified.

   a Crisis management: reasoning, trying to get bullies to understand how their victims feel; peer group pressure; formal procedures – for example, the investigating adult asks the children involved the same questions (who? what? when? etc.), and each child's response (e.g. feeling sorry, denying it happened) is used as the basis for deciding what individual action will be taken.

b Intervention: certain situations are high risk (e.g. changing schools, learning difficulties, gifted students, race, physical appearance). Strategies include appointing a 'buddy' to help the new student, the child with a learning difficulty etc. (but choose carefully – not all children are suited to this role); open discussion and education within the whole setting (e.g. nursery, school) about bullying, individual differences, etc.

✦ Preventative (short- and long-term): planning ahead to discourage bullying:

a have a policy on bullying (including rules and consequences)

b teach about bullying and other antisocial behaviour

c ensure that children and parents know that bullying is unacceptable

d identify 'hot spots' (e.g. where children cannot be seen easily), and either supervise these areas or modify/eliminate them

e keep records of episodes and strategies used and their success/failure

f provide staff development in victim support and management strategies

g supervise ALL children in the playground/at break-time

h look at the emphasis given to activities (e.g. competitiveness is not always bad, but it can sometimes be over emphasised).

Further information

www.bullying.co.uk (accessed 20 September 2005)

▶▶ Central Auditory Processing Disorder (CAPD)

A CAPD is a *HEARING* **impairment**, but it does not show up as a hearing loss on an audiogram. It affects the hearing system beyond the ear, where meaningful messages are separated from non-essential background sound and delivered with good clarity to the brain.

Causes

Often the exact cause is not known, but any of the following may be related to a CAPD:

✦ **genetic** – CAPD or similar difficulties often run in families

✦ **neurological** dysfunction

✦ birth difficulties (e.g. lack of oxygen)

✦ brain injury.

Characteristics

Any of the following characteristics may apply:

✦ seems not to hear very well despite normal hearing (e.g. slow to respond when spoken to)

✦ possible *PREMATURITY*

✦ probable history of repeated *MIDDLE EAR INFECTIONS*

✦ seems not to understand questions, has difficulty following instructions (particularly in noisy, larger group settings)

✦ average intellectual **aptitude** (as measured by an **IQ test**)

✦ *LANGUAGE AND SPEECH* delay

✦ difficulty understanding multiple meanings in words (e.g. 'It cost an arm and a leg')

✦ disorganised, easily distracted, slow to start/finish tasks

✦ possible behavioural problems (inattention, distracts others)

✦ difficulty with friendships (reading body language, gauging others' feelings).

Diagnosis

Evaluation should be multidisciplinary and should consist of developmental screening, medical assessment (including an audiogram and an ear, nose and throat check-up), parent interview, behaviour checklists, psycho-educational *TESTING* (including IQ, visual and auditory information-processing skills) and speech and language assessment.

Strategies

✦ Allow a little extra time for the CAPD child to reply, follow directions, etc.

✦ Break down sequences of information and tasks into smaller steps.

✦ Get the child's attention before giving information (e.g. have a recognised cue as a signal), but avoid singling out and embarrassing the child.

✦ Encourage good eye contact when giving verbal information (i.e. make sure the child is looking at the speaker).

✦ Manage noise in the environment (e.g. echoes, scraping chairs).

✦ Practise listening skills, reading body language etc. (this could benefit the whole group/class).

✦ Provide specific language skills sessions (e.g. vocabulary, word meanings, listening skills).

✦ Put the CAPD child with another child who is 'good' at listening.

✦ Repeat important information for the child and have the child verbalise it back.

✦ Seat the child where there is as little background noise as possible and in the area closest to whoever is talking/giving instructions.

✦ Use **multi-sensory** teaching (e.g. pair spoken information with visual information or motor activities – hands-on, manipulative, 'doing' tasks).

Further information

LDOnLine, www.ldonline.org (search term CAPD) (accessed 20 September 2005)

Auditory Processing Disorder UK, www.apduk.org (accessed 20 September 2005)

➤➤ Cerebral Palsy

Cerebral Palsy (CP) is a medical condition that affects muscle control (cerebral refers to the brain and palsy refers to poor control). There are several types of CP; characteristics vary in severity and from one person to the next, and they may change over time. Some people with CP also have additional medical or other **disorders** (e.g. **seizures**, **intellectual impairment**), but having CP does not automatically imply learning or other difficulties, and children with CP are often able to participate in mainstream care and education.

Causes

Cerebral Palsy is caused by an injury to the brain before, during or shortly after birth. In many cases, it is not known for certain what caused the brain injury. Lack of oxygen at birth (e.g. due to *PREMATURITY*) is one known cause.

Types

✦ Spastic Cerebral Palsy is the most common form, affecting 70–80 per cent of children who suffer from CP. It is characterised by stiff, jerky movements, caused by muscles which are too tight (high tone). Sufferers have particular difficulties moving from one body position to another, or letting go of an object held in the hand.

✦ Ataxic Cerebral Palsy affects an estimated 5–10 per cent of children with CP. It is characterised by poor coordination and loose muscle tone (low tone). Children have poor balance, and look very unsteady and shaky. Shakiness can be more pronounced in fine-motor movements (e.g. turning the page of a book).

✦ Athetoid or dyskinetic Cerebral Palsy affects about 10–20 per cent of children with CP. It is characterised by a mixture of muscle tone (too tight/too loose). The child has trouble holding the body in an upright, steady position for sitting or walking. There are often lots of involuntary and unintentional movements of the face, arms and upper body.

✦ Mixed Cerebral Palsy is characterised by the muscle tone being too low in some muscles and too high in other muscles.

Treatment

Children with severe CP might be unable to walk and may need extensive and lifelong care, whereas a child with mild CP might only be slightly awkward and require no special assistance. Where there are associated disorders or problems (e.g. *EPILEPSY*, intellectual impairment), special needs support or medication may be needed, and *PHYSIOTHERAPISTS*, *SPEECH AND LANGUAGE THERAPISTS* and *OCCUPATIONAL THERAPISTS* are often used to assist the child in developing and strengthening their speech and physical coordination.

Further information

Cerebral Palsy Information Central, www.geocities.com/aneecp (accessed 20 September 2005)

Scope, www.scope.org.uk (accessed 20 September 2005)

www.psychnet-uk.com/dsm_iv/cerebral_palsy.htm (accessed 20 September 2005)

➤➤ Child abuse

There are legal definitions of abuse and maltreatment, various legal procedures and a range of service professionals who become involved when abuse is suspected. Concerns for a child's health and safety (due to abuse or anything else) should be referred to an appropriate service.

Listed here are some indicators that suggest that a child's health and/or safety may be at risk.

Emotional abuse

Physical indicators include:

+ eating **disorders** (e.g. anorexia)
+ delays in language or motor skills development
+ weight or height notably below norm
+ nervous/stress reactions (e.g. stomach aches, *STUTTERING/STAMMERING*).

Behavioural indicators include:

+ ritualistic behaviour (e.g. rocking)
+ cruelty to others (children, animals); seeming to get pleasure from hurting others or being hurt themselves
+ age-inappropriate behaviours (e.g. *BED-WETTING*)
+ extremes of behaviour (e.g. too compliant/demanding, withdrawn/aggressive).

Neglect

Physical indicators include:

+ poor hygiene (e.g. head lice, body odour)
+ odd clothing; missing basic items (e.g. underwear, shoes); over/underdressed for weather
+ untreated injury or illness
+ no immunisations
+ signs of prolonged exposure to the elements (e.g. excessive sunburn, insect bites)
+ height and weight **significant**ly below age level

Behavioural indicators include:

◆ chronic school absences

◆ chronic hunger, tiredness, lethargy

◆ collecting leftover food

◆ assuming adult responsibilities

◆ reporting no caretaker at home.

Physical abuse

Physical indicators include:

◆ unexplained bruises and welts on the face, throat, upper arms, buttocks, thighs or lower back, in patterns/shapes (e.g. suggesting a belt buckle, an electric cord); these regularly appear after a break (e.g. weekend), in various stages of healing

◆ 'dot' burn marks (like cigarettes), especially on palms, soles of feet, abdomen, buttocks

◆ blotchy, reddish marks on buttocks, soles of feet, palms

◆ burns in the shape of common household utensils

◆ rope burns

◆ infected burns (suggesting delay in treating them).

Behavioural indicators include:

◆ behavioural extremes (withdrawal, aggression, regressive behaviours such as thumb-sucking)

◆ inappropriate/excessive fear of parent or caretaker, of going home

◆ unbelievable or inconsistent explanation for injuries (by the child or the adult)

◆ unusual stillness, watchfulness, shyness, wariness of physical contact.

Sexual abuse

Physical indicators include:

◆ torn, bloodstained underclothes

◆ frequent, unexplained sore throats; urinary infections

◆ pain and irritation of the genitals

◆ bruises or bleeding from external genitalia, vagina or anal region

◆ difficulty walking or sitting.

Behavioural indicators include:

✦ child talks about it (e.g. in play activities)
✦ regressive behaviours (e.g. thumb-sucking, fear of the dark)
✦ *SLEEP PROBLEMS*
✦ unusual interest in sexual matters
✦ child avoids undressing or wants to wear extra layers of clothes
✦ sudden decline in school performance, increased absences.

Further information

www.childabuse.com (accessed 20 September 2005)

ChildLine, www.childline.org.uk (accessed 20 September 2005)

National Society for the Prevention of Cruelty to Children, www.nspcc.org.uk (accessed 20 September 2005)

➤➤ Children in care: Foster care

Children are placed 'in care' when there are concerns for their physical, mental and emotional health and safety. Options include residential care, foster care and supervised care with the birth parent/s or family.

Surveys in the last few years indicate that at any one time in the UK about 60,000 children (from birth to 18 years) are in care, and that approximately 2/3 are in foster care and 40 per cent are under 10 years of age.

Foster care

Fostering is caring for children who cannot live with their birth parent/s. The birth parent/s continue to hold legal parental responsibility, although this is often shared by a local agency (e.g. child welfare office).

Various foster care placements are offered, and while the terminology may differ among service providers, here are some typical examples:

+ short-term: while mother is in hospital, for example
+ permanent: through to adulthood or until placed for adoption
+ emergency: with a longer-term placement to be arranged as soon as possible
+ respite care: children continue to live at home, but carers offer regular 'breaks' (e.g. weekends, holidays)
+ remand fostering: young people placed in the care of a local authority because of a serious legal offence
+ parent and child: placements for young people prior to and following the birth of their baby
+ assessment: care of a child while social services workers assess long-term needs
+ permanent disability: full-time permanent placements for children with severe/multiple disabilities.

Associated issues

Government and other agency studies in the UK show that, compared to children within a family unit, children in foster care are more vulnerable to a range of difficulties, including:

+ attention and concentration problems
+ conduct **disorders** (e.g. oppositional defiant disorder, aggression)
+ emotional disorders (e.g. low **self-esteem**)
+ learning difficulties

◆ mental disorders (e.g. **anxiety**, *DEPRESSION*)
◆ poor social skills and lack of peer friendships (often due to changes of school when a care placement is changed)
◆ school absenteeism
◆ school failure (e.g. poor results in UK Key Stage tests at ages 7, 11 and 14, relative to the general population)
◆ teasing, *BULLYING*.

Early years providers and schools need to have positive, realistic expectations for children in care (as for any child, it is hoped); they need to be aware of what it means to be in care, be sympathetic but not differentiate unnecessarily; and they should be alert to the problems that children in care have a particular tendency to experience (without assuming problems will arise), and ask for advice as needed.

Further information

British Association for Adoption & Fostering, www.baaf.org.uk (accessed 20 September 2005)

➤➤ Cleft lip and palate: An overview

In the early stages of pregnancy, separate areas of the face develop individually and then join together. If some parts do not join properly, a cleft (a split/separation), of varying type and severity, remains.

Clefting can now sometimes be identified by ultrasound prior to the baby's birth.

Cleft palate

If you feel the top of the inside of your mouth with your tongue, first at the back and then at the front, you'll notice the difference between the soft and hard palate. A cleft in the palate can range from just an opening at the back of the soft palate (towards the throat) to a nearly complete separation of the roof of the mouth (affecting both soft and hard palate). A baby with a cleft palate as well as a small lower jaw (Pierre Robin sequence) can have difficulties breathing easily.

Cleft lip

This looks like a split in the lip, but it is actually an opening in the upper lip between the mouth and nose. It extends up and into the nose, varying from a slight indentation in the coloured portion of the lip to complete separation, and can be on one side of the lip (unilateral cleft) or both sides (bilateral).

A cleft in the gum can also occur, again ranging from a small notch to complete division of the gum.

Causes

The most common cause appears to be a combination of **genetics** and environment, although some children can be born with a cleft without any family history. The risk of a cleft condition depends on several factors (e.g. how many other people in the family have a cleft condition, the severity of the clefts and how close the family connection is between family members with clefts).

Associated problems

Facial deformity, increased susceptibility to colds, **otitis media** (*MIDDLE EAR INFECTIONS*), *HEARING* loss, speech defects, a larger than average number of dental cavities, and missing/extra/malformed teeth.

A cleft lip can make it more difficult for an infant to suck on a nipple and can also cause formula or breast-milk to accidentally 'spill' into the nasal cavity. In some cases, until they have reconstructive surgery, children may need to wear a prosthetic (false) palate to help them eat properly.

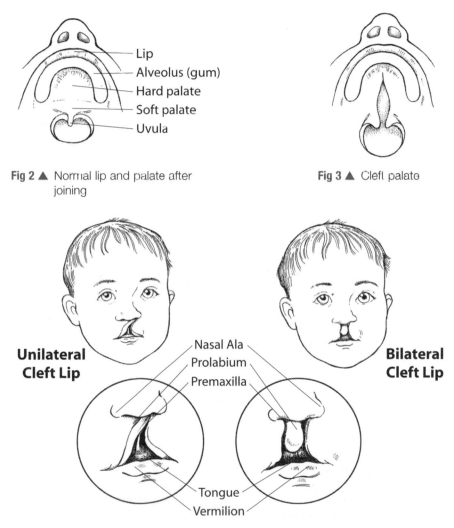

Lip
Alveolus (gum)
Hard palate
Soft palate
Uvula

Fig 2 ▲ Normal lip and palate after joining

Fig 3 ▲ Cleft palate

Unilateral Cleft Lip

Bilateral Cleft Lip

Nasal Ala
Prolabium
Premaxilla

Tongue
Vermilion

Fig 4 ▲ Unilateral cleft lip and bilateral cleft lip

Further information

Cleft Lip and Palate Association, www.clapa.com (accessed 20 September 2005)

➤➤ Cleft lip and palate: Treatment

Surgery

+ Lip surgery: the cleft is usually closed when the healthy infant is about 3 months old, to help the face develop with minimal scarring.
+ Palate bone grafting: a small amount of bone is taken from one place (e.g. hip, leg) and inserted into the cleft area. This is most successful in patients aged between about 6 and 10 years.
+ Plastic surgery: this can improve appearance, and is often considered when the child is around 14–18 years old.

Dentistry/orthodontics

+ Missing teeth can be replaced by moving adjacent teeth, by dental bridges and by metallic implants.
+ Children with clefts need the same dental care as other children (e.g. regular brushing and flossing).

Speech therapy

+ Some children may have soft, nasal voices and/or their speech may be difficult to understand. A *SPEECH AND LANGUAGE THERAPIST* evaluates *LANGUAGE AND SPEECH* development and the sounds and words being attempted. This helps determine if speech exercises and/or further surgery are needed. Speech therapy may be needed for several years, and early intervention provides the best prognosis.
+ **Oro-motor** functioning can be affected (e.g. slight drooling), and *OCCUPATIONAL THERAPISTS* can provide activities to increase sensory awareness and control.

Special devices

+ Infants in particular can have difficulties feeding, swallowing, and so on, and special aids (e.g. special teats) can help.
+ There are also aids to help in dental care (e.g. a 'toothette' – a soft, mouthwash-containing sponge on a handle – which can later be switched to a soft children's toothbrush).

Counselling

Children with facial differences are at risk of low **self-esteem**, lack of confidence and teasing, and the role of parents and other adults is critical.

✦ Self-esteem. From a very early age, children look to see how others react to their difference, developing **self-image** accordingly. The family/school photo album can help the child accept a facial difference as normal, since it shows pride in the child regardless of the cleft. It also provides opportunities for the child, or other children, to ask questions about the condition. Explanations need to be truthful but age-appropriate.

✦ Negative social interactions. Children with facial difficulties often have to deal with teasing and they need help to deal with this. Talking about it, asking the child what s/he would like to say and then helping the child to practise is one way of helping. Talking with children as a group about individual differences of any kind can also encourage tolerance and openness.

✦ Social-emotional problems. The teen years can be especially difficult for someone with a physical difference and *PSYCHOTHERAPY* can offer valuable support.

➤➤ Cognitive Development

Cognition describes things like thinking, memory, mental imagery, reasoning and understanding. Thus all of us have a number of 'cognitions'. Cognitive development is the way in which various cognitions emerge, change and mature over time.

There are several theories of how cognitions develop (perhaps the most famous being that of Jean *PIAGET*), and one of the key issues for people working with young children is understanding the multitude of terms and meanings that are used, and which can sometimes confuse rather than clarify.

Terminology

+ Cognitive psychology is the study of cognitive processes – how we think, understand, reason, and so on.

+ Perception is the process that takes in, and orders, the information we see, hear, taste, smell, feel and, sometimes, sense. Thus we have visual perceptions, auditory perceptions, motor perceptions, and so on. These processes lead to the formation of concepts. Perceptions can be influenced by age, experience, physical and mental health, mood, and so on.

+ A concept is an 'internal' set of ideas or properties that define something, a fixed idea/image of what it is. Concepts can be concrete (when I say 'houses', what do you 'see') or **abstract** (what is 'justice' or 'liberty'). Age, experience and culture can influence our concepts.

+ Mental imagery is the impression, or the picture, we call up in our minds, without it actually being in front of us. It can be a visual, auditory, taste or feel image and can be quite specific (e.g. a chair) or more subtle (e.g. summer).

+ Memory can be described as: processing information (perceiving) and storing it for later use; the storage system itself; or the meaning of the information (concepts).

+ Memory can be visual, auditory, motor, visual-motor, and so on, depending on the perceptions involved. Moreover, most of us are better at some kinds of memory than others, which is why some children can remember information they have heard better than information they have seen. This is why **multi-sensory** experiences are so important, because they take into consideration the range of children's individual learning preferences, strengths and weaknesses.

✦ Memory can also be further categorised as long-term memory, short-term memory and working memory.

    a   Long-term memory is the storage of information/concepts for any period of time, including a lifetime, and has seemingly unlimited capacity.

    b   Short-term memory is where information first enters the cognitive process, and can hold up to 7 items. Information lasts 18–20 seconds, and gives us a chance to 'use it' (e.g. solve a problem with it there and then, or send it to the long-term memory for later use), or 'lose it' (discard it completely, so that it is never really known).

    c   Working memory represents the middle ground between long-term memory and short-term memory, where the job of 'use it or lose it' takes place. It is when we say, 'Just a minute, I'm thinking!'

✦ Memories are recollections of information and they are not always exactly the same as the concepts that were first stored. Details can be omitted or even added (to make sense of the memory or maybe to apply it to a current situation).

✦ Learning is the process that brings about a relatively permanent change in what we know and understand and how we behave. The end result is we 'learned' it. There are several theories about how it comes about:

    a   Behaviourism holds that learning happens as a result of experience. If a behaviour is reinforced (e.g. attracts a response that the person likes), it is likely to be repeated, and if this behaviour-response 'pattern' happens often enough, then the behaviour will become more or less permanent and the person will have learned it. Conversely, if a behaviour consistently earns a response the person does not like, then that behaviour will change or disappear altogether. Early theories of behaviourism rejected the 'mind' as important to learning, since it could not be measured, but current interpretations of behaviourism (e.g. *BEHAVIOUR MANAGEMENT*) see cognition as extremely important.

    b   Observational learning/social learning holds that reinforcement is important but that it is not enough on its own. Social Learning Theory maintains that we learn by observing and copying others whom we admire, and by doing what we see others do to solve problems, not just by being rewarded or punished for a behaviour. We also learn by observing the consequences of other people's behaviour, deciding if we like those consequences or not, and, therefore, whether we will copy that behaviour.

c Humanism says that one cannot generalise about how people learn because each person is an individual, with their own interests, abilities and motivations for learning. It acknowledges that cognitions occur and are important, but that they are unique to each person and thus should not/cannot be categorised or measured scientifically.

✦ **Intelligence** is the ability to make sense of a situation, to understand it, to organise it and to do something appropriate to the situation. It includes the ability to analyse, to adapt, to learn and to survive. Some people think that it can be measured and that intelligence is what is measured. Others think that such *TESTING* captures only one aspect of intelligence, or that it is not actually measuring it at all.

✦ Intellect is that part of our thinking that tries to remove any emotional factors from a situation and understand it and respond to it in a logical way.

Further information

Hayes, N. and Stratton, P., *A Student's Dictionary of Psychology*, 4th edn, Hodder Arnold, London, 2003.

www.learningandteaching.info/learning (accessed 20 September 2005)

➤➤ Death and dying: Children's perceptions

Children's developmental understanding

Developmental stages are an important aid to helping children deal with death, because they offer guidelines as to how they are likely to be thinking, what they are likely to be able to understand, how they are likely to react to their own distress, as well as to that of others, and how they can be helped through a difficult time. As with all guidelines, however, keep children's individual differences and circumstances in mind.

✦ Newborn to 3 years sense when their family routine is disrupted, and when those around them are upset. They react emotionally to the absence of a significant person, especially a mother figure.

Reactions include changes in sleeping, eating and mood (e.g. unusual irritability).

✦ From 3 to 5 years, children demonstrate misunderstanding of verbal explanations, and may take words literally (e.g. we 'lost' Grandma). They have little or no concept of time, the future, the life cycle, and so on, so there is little or no understanding of what death is. They may be afraid that dead people are cold or hungry in the grave.

They gradually begin to develop the idea that death is about changing from one kind of 'person' to another (e.g. a 'spirit', an 'angel', a 'memory in your heart').

Reactions include frightening dreams; repeated questions about death; reverting to babyish behaviours (for comfort, to go back to the way things were, to take some time out while they try to understand); play-acting events to try to understand them; connecting events that do not really relate (e.g. 'Aunt Sally died from a stomach ache. Daddy says he has a stomach ache – maybe he will die, too').

✦ From 6 to 9 years, children may view death as 'accidental' (e.g. it just comes and takes people away). They tend to believe that their behaviours can cause catastrophic events (e.g. may worry that naughtiness or bad thoughts cause death, divorce, etc.), but they are increasingly able to accept logical explanations against this. They have a more realistic concept of time and the life cycle and can understand the finality of death; they try to give it meaning (e.g. death is 'the devil', 'God', a 'ghost').

Reactions include distress, confusion, guilt because of wishful thinking ('I wish he would die!'), harsh words ('You'll be the death of me yet!') or not doing something ('I didn't help Grandpa sweep the leaves and now he's dead'); **anxiety** about parents' health (compulsive caregiving, attempts to be good so they do not cause something bad to happen); obsession with the causes of death and what happens to the body; seemingly inappropriate giggling, joking (to create distance from the upset); a fantasy relationship with the dead person (in an attempt to keep them alive).

✦ From 9 to 12 years, the child begins to develop an understanding of death as irreversible, and experience fears for their own mortality and that of others. They are capable of projecting into the future (may express feelings of 'helplessness' against 'fate'). Their increasing independence means they may not want to open up to parents, preferring an 'outsider' (e.g. teacher, friend).

Reactions include anger directed at various people (e.g. self, others, the person who died); reluctance to talk about the death because it upsets others (e.g. makes Mum cry) or because it makes them afraid (if I don't talk about it, it will go away); may be overprotective of family members (to try to stop them from dying too); focus on the gruesome details of dying and death (externalising in this way gives the child some sense of control).

How to help

Although children's needs differ with age and stage, there are some common threads of advice:

✦ maintain routines

✦ set behaviour limits, but be a little flexible

✦ share information at the child's level of understanding and in 'doses' that the child can manage

✦ when telling a child that someone has died, make sure the word 'died' is used – euphemisms are confusing

✦ talk about and accept feelings (e.g. it is okay to be angry, sad, not want to talk about it)

✦ be available

✦ admit that you do not have all the answers

✦ know your own feelings and beliefs so that you can talk as naturally as possible with children.

The healing process

After someone close dies, some children may act younger than their age (e.g. use 'baby talk', want more cuddles), and they are likely to feel sadness off and on for some time (and often at unexpected moments). They may also want to talk a lot about the person or to create 'fantasies' about them. This is all part of the healing process.

Progress needs to be monitored, however, and, at times, the child may need help to move on. Talking about it being normal to feel sad, to wish it had not happened, and so on, keeps things out in the open and helps avoid pent-up emotions.

Things like helping to choose a memorial plaque or headstone and the wording on it can also help, as can photos and mementos, continuing traditions (birthdays, etc.) and special 'celebrations'.

Behavioural extremes may signal the need for particular help; for example, aggression, frequent panic attacks, inability/unwillingness to socialise, continued denial of the death or feeling responsible for it, notable decline in school behaviour and performance, prolonged withdrawal, loss of interest in daily activities, poor sleep, loss of appetite.

▶▶ Death and grieving: Talking with children

When a death is expected, there is an opportunity to talk about it and time to understand it before everyone is grief-stricken. Children may not want to talk about it, however, or they may want to ask about concrete things (e.g. is lying in the ground scary, cold, lonely?), and it is important for adults to be prepared. Nor do children usually sit down and discuss for hours. They run up, ask some of the hardest questions in the world, want an answer there and then, and, after a couple of minutes, they are off again to play.

Reading books together is a good way of talking about death, and local libraries are good sources of age-appropriate material.

When telling a child that someone has died, a familiar person, close to the child, should be the one to do so. Find a place that will not be disturbed, stay with the facts and avoid misleading explanations. Be patient, because it can take a while for children to react. They do not always have the language skills to verbalise concerns right away, or they may feel too confused or embarrassed to ask.

Should children attend funeral services?

The rituals surrounding death vary greatly (e.g. from religion to religion, culture to culture), and deciding whether or not the child should attend is not always an option. When it is, it is important to remember individual differences and circumstances. Some children may feel left out if they do not attend, but they should not be forced to participate if they do not want to. The service can formalise events (make it 'real'), allow open emotions, help bring a sense of closure and enable family and friends to offer support, but it can also frighten and confuse.

When attending services, children should be:
✦ prepared for what happens, what they might see (e.g. what the coffin looks like, that adults might cry)
✦ catered for (e.g. when a parent is grieving, the child may need another caring adult to comfort them, to answer their questions)
✦ allowed to participate (e.g. choose a song for the service, place a flower or a drawing in the coffin)
✦ encouraged to talk, draw or play after the service, to help release emotions.

Further information

Beyond Indigo, changing the way you feel about grief and loss, www.beyondindigo.com (accessed 20 September 2005) and www.beyondindigo.com/children/

➤➤ Depression in children and adolescents

Most adults and children feel low or 'down' occasionally, but when these feelings persist and start to interfere with daily life, it can become clinical depression. Research suggests that depression probably affects 1 in every 200 children under 12 years and 2–3 in every 100 teenagers.

Risk factors

✦ personal events (e.g. *DIVORCE AND SEPARATION, DEATH AND GRIEVING, CHILD ABUSE, BULLYING*)
✦ too many changes happening too quickly
✦ stress (e.g. school failure)
✦ family history
✦ younger boys and girls are at equal risk, but adolescent girls are twice as vulnerable as boys
✦ a link with chemical changes in the mood control centre of the brain.

Categories and symptoms

Major Depressive Disorder

Typically, 5 or more symptoms must exist for at least 2 weeks to consider a diagnosis of Major Depressive Disorder. Symptoms may include:

✦ appetite changes
✦ avoidance of friends, family, regular activities
✦ changes in sleep pattern (e.g. sleeping too little/too much)
✦ difficulty with relationships (peers, family)
✦ feeling persistently unhappy, lonely, hopeless
✦ feelings of guilt, self-loathing
✦ frequent minor health complaints (e.g. headaches, stomach aches)
✦ increased school absence, poor school performance
✦ moody, irritable, easily upset
✦ poor concentration
✦ poor hygiene and personal appearance
✦ reckless behaviour, risk-taking
✦ tiredness, lack of energy (sometimes despite plenty of sleep).

Bipolar Disorder

Bipolar disorder (manic-depressive illness) beginning in childhood or early adolescence is rare, but where it occurs it is thought that it might be a different and more severe form of the disorder. Symptoms may include:

✦ agitation; talks too much, too fast; changes topics too quickly; cannot be interrupted

✦ ability to go with very little or no sleep for days without tiring

✦ excessive risk-taking

✦ hyper-sexual thoughts, behaviours, language

✦ overinflated **self-esteem**

✦ overly focused or overly distracted

✦ severe mood changes (extremely irritable to overly silly, elated).

Dysthymia, Unspecified Depression and Adjustment Disorder

Dysthymia is when a depressed mood persists for a year or more, accompanied by at least two other symptoms of major depressive disorder, with an increased risk of developing other depressive disorders.

Unspecified depression includes depression not quite severe enough to be diagnosed as major depression, or ongoing, moderate depression which has not been present long enough for a diagnosis of dysthymia.

Adjustment disorder, with depression, describes depression occurring in response to a major life stress or crisis.

Diagnosis

Concerns should be referred to an appropriate professional (e.g. psychologist, psychiatrist).

Treatment

This may take the form of *PSYCHOTHERAPY*, or medication may be considered for children and adolescents in some instances (e.g. severe symptoms that would prevent effective psychotherapy). A combination of psychotherapy and medication can often be recommended.

Further information

American Academy of Child and Adolescent Psychiatry, www.aacap.org (accessed 20 September 2005)

➤➤ Diabetes (Type 1)

Diabetes may take the form of Type 1 or Type 2 diabetes, with Type 1 rarer in general, but the most common in children. In both types, insufficient insulin is produced to keep blood sugar (glucose) at the right level. Glucose is needed for the brain, nervous system and energy.

Research indicates a threefold increase in childhood diabetes (Type 1) over the last 30 years and an increase in Type 2 diabetes in children (with a possible link to increased child and adolescent obesity).

Characteristics (Type 1)

✦ Insulin-dependent
✦ It is an auto-immune disease (the body's **immune system** attacks one of its own organs).
✦ Insulin-producing cells are destroyed.
✦ The insulin-producing gland is damaged.
✦ It is more severe than Type 2.
✦ Family history increases risk.
✦ Environmental and **genetic** factors may interact.

The process

Glucose circulates in the body via blood cells with the help of insulin, which is produced in the pancreas by beta cells. The auto-immune disease gradually destroys these cells and insulin production goes down and down. Without enough insulin to move the glucose round the body, the glucose does not get used up, glucose levels in the blood get higher and higher (hyperglycaemia) and eventually glucose spills over into the urine and is lost (and therefore glucose levels go down, often too low, causing hypoglycaemia).

Symptoms

Symptoms may include:
✦ excessive hunger and/or thirst
✦ frequent urination
✦ skin and genital area infections
✦ weakness, tiredness
✦ weight loss.

Treatment

✦ Regular insulin injections: each child will have an insulin routine that must be followed. There are various methods e.g.: syringe injection, insulin pumps (a small unit connected to a thin tube inserted under the skin), pen injectors (can be used through clothing).

✦ Blood-sugar monitoring: a drop of blood is put on a test strip and checked for glucose levels, sometimes several times a day. A lancing kit (blade, test strip, container for disposing of blade) and a glucose meter are required.

✦ Meal planning: meals and snacks are worked out carefully and taken at set times.

✦ Sensible exercise levels: exercise uses blood sugar, so it may need to be balanced with snacks beforehand.

At day-care, school, and so on, staff must be informed that a child has diabetes and told about particular requirements (e.g. insulin schedule, equipment needed, diet, symptoms of hypoglycaemia and what to do). Moreover, children with diabetes can feel embarrassed or resentful about their condition, about injecting, having to have special meals, and so on, and may need particular social and emotional understanding.

Further information

Children with Diabetes, www.childrenwithdiabetes.com (accessed 20 September 2005)

www.netdoctor.co.uk (search term: diabetes in children) (accessed 20 September 2005)

➤➤ Divorce and separation

Divorce is the legal ending of a marriage; separation takes place between a married or unmarried couple who were cohabiting and who have lived apart for a specified amount of time – it does not always involve legal proceedings.

Knowing something about what children need and understand at different **developmental stages** can help to make discussions about divorce and/or separation more meaningful.

From birth to 12 months, infants:
+ develop trust from knowing that needs will be taken care of (e.g. hunger, a wet nappy)
+ begin to distinguish tones of voice by about 4 months
+ are 'in tune' with physical tension in carers (because of frequent physical contact)
+ develop 'separation anxiety' and 'fear of strangers' at around 8 months
+ display definite people preferences by 12 months
+ are likely to become distressed and fretful when 'preferred people' communicate tension (e.g. angry voices) or they are no longer around.

From 1 to 3 years, children:
+ begin walking, talking and exploring (but need the significant people in their lives to run back to when they get frightened)
+ perceive any changes as threatening to them personally (**egocentricity**)
+ may exhibit an increase in attention-seeking behaviour (crying, tantrums), *SLEEP PROBLEMS* and fretful, clinging behaviour, caused by upset.

From 3 to 5 years, children:
+ talk coherently and are physically active
+ develop a sense of time
+ are egocentric (tend to think they cause events)
+ have trouble distinguishing between fantasy and reality, with vivid imaginations and fears
+ can sense upsets and tensions but cannot understand the 'why' and become anxious
+ when upset, may become clingy or revert to infant behaviours (in an attempt to go back to the way things were), have sleep difficulties or nightmares, and may be unusually aggressive and anxious.

From 6 to 12 years, children:

◆ develop stronger intellectual skills and awareness

◆ are still dependent socially, emotionally and physically, and often feel extreme loss when a divorce occurs

◆ may feel guilt (they did something wrong to make Mum/Dad leave) or will fear rejection (they will be abandoned)

◆ wish, typically, for parents to reunite

◆ may blame one parent.

Strategies

Maintain routines and set behaviour limits (although some flexibility may be needed). Answer 'why' questions simply but truthfully, and avoid casting blame in front of children. Listen to the outraged feelings of older children.

Further information

Joseph Rowntree Foundation, www.jrf.org.uk/knowledge/findings (search term: children divorce) (accessed 20 September 2005)

►► Down's Syndrome

Down's Syndrome is a **genetic impairment** usually immediately identifiable at birth because of distinctive physical characteristics. Down's Syndrome is a lifelong condition, but various treatments can help with the problems associated with it.

Cause

Normally, each cell in the human body contains 46 **chromosomes**, in 2 sets of 23 (23 from each parent), and these paired chromosomes decide our inherited characteristics. Children with Down's Syndrome most often have an abnormality on the 21st pair of chromosomes, where there are 3 instead of 2 (thus making 47 altogether). This is called Trisomy 21.

No one knows exactly why this occurs, and no one is to blame. While there does seem to be a link between the mother's age and higher risk, 80 per cent of children with Down's Syndrome are born to mothers under the age of 35 (because the birth rate is higher among younger women).

Characteristics

These include:
+ below-average birth weight and length
+ floppy muscle tone (hypotonia) that usually improves with age
+ a rather flat face
+ eyes that slant upwards
+ the epicanthic fold (a vertical fold of skin between the upper and lower eye-lids, in the inner corner of the eye)
+ rather large tongue in a smallish mouth, often causing the tongue to protrude
+ broad hands, short fingers, little finger curves in
+ the palm may have a single line/crease across it
+ a deep groove between the first and second toes and running along the foot.

Difficulties at birth

These vary from infant to infant, but can include:
+ difficulty sucking, swallowing
+ breathing, lung, heart abnormalities
+ poor muscle tone and strength
+ weight loss due to feeding problems.

Developmental difficulties

Health problems, developmental delay and special needs are common; for example:

✦ heart defects (affecting 40–50 per cent of children with Down's Syndrome)

✦ tendency to chest and lung infections

✦ poor temperature control and dry skin

✦ up to 2 to 3 years' delay in sitting/standing/walking

✦ first words are often delayed by 1–2 years; sometimes **oro-motor** functioning is impaired and speech is not very clear

✦ delays in independent self-help skills (e.g. toileting, dressing)

✦ children with Down's Syndrome learn in the same way as other children, but are usually delayed

✦ some children have **significant intellectual impairment.**

Treatment and therapies

Children with Down's Syndrome may have to have surgery, particularly for heart conditions, and can also have corrective surgery for characteristic facial differences. Most children also need various kinds of professional input (e.g. medical supervision, speech and language therapy, **applied behaviour analysis (ABA)**, play therapy).

Further information

Down's Syndrome Association, www.downs-syndrome.org.uk (accessed 20 September 2005)

➤➤ Drawing

Various studies of children's drawings have provided a profile of characteristics that reveal much about overall development, particularly in skills related to drawing (e.g. fine-motor skills, visual perception). Children's drawings have also been used to estimate **non-verbal intellectual ability** (e.g. Goodenough-Harris Draw-A-Person Test). However, factors such as socio-economic level and cultural norms have also been shown to have a **significant** effect on scores, so an interpretation of children's drawings alone should not be considered diagnostic.

Drawing: developmental stages

Scribble

+ about 15 months to 3 years
+ mixture of gross-motor grasps (e.g. fist, **horizontal palmar grasp**)
+ changes/experiments with grip and working hand
+ random scribbles and playful exploration of materials
+ uncontrolled scribbling gradually becomes controlled
+ as control increases, movements become slower and marks include wavy lines, looped lines and overlaid circles

+ begins to name and point to things they can 'see' in the scribble
+ attempts to draw basic geometric shapes
+ children begin talking about marks, colours, etc.

Fig 5 ▲

Diagrammatic/combined/pre-schematic stage

+ about 2–4 years
+ tripod grasp emerges (thumb and forefinger grasp pencil just above point, with pencil resting on middle finger – see figure 12, p. 106)
+ occasional hand-swapping and grasp changes
+ children tend to use their favourite colours rather than choose realistic colours (e.g. purple fish)
+ stick people or 'tadpole' figures (large head on tiny body with extended arms) are usual

- geometric shapes become more precise and are used to make pictures of real objects (e.g. a house, a car)
- objects float in space (e.g. the stars are over here, the moon down there, here is 'me' – probably dead-centre, given the child's **egocentricity**!).

Aggregate/schematic stage

Fig 6 ▲

- about 5–8 years
- tripod grasp is more dynamic/controlled (e.g. can adjust pencil position without changing grasp)
- controls drawing surface with non-dominant hand
- develops a set way of drawing (e.g. draws a fish exactly the same way every time)
- more realistic use of colour, often based on stereotypes (e.g. blue sky, yellow sun)
- ground and sky lines are drawn in (pictures no longer 'float')
- drawings of figures show better proportion, more detail, gender differences
- create stories to go with drawings or drawings have themes.

Pictorial/pre-teen stage

Fig 7 ▲

- about 9–12 years
- greater detail in drawings
- hand preference and dynamic tripod grasp established, giving greater control over detail, size, and so on
- perspective emerges
- try to create very realistic images and get frustrated when it 'doesn't look right'
- the 'I can't draw' syndrome starts to emerge.

Fig 8 ▲

Further information

Susan Donley Learning Design, www.learningdesign.com/Portfolio/DrawDev/kiddrawing.html (accessed 20 September 2005)

➤➤ Dyscalculia

Dyscalculia affects maths ability. While it is a lifelong **disorder**, it does not necessarily mean a severe handicap. Dyscalculia can be primarily quantitative (main difficulties lie with counting and calculations), qualitative (understanding concepts) and intermediate (numbers or other symbols). It can cause difficulties with:

✦ mental maths, everyday use of money (e.g. working out change at the shop)

✦ processes (e.g. subtraction, multiplication) and concepts (e.g. place value/tens and units)

✦ remembering concepts and rules from one day or one setting to the next

✦ directions, reading maps, telling time, understanding mechanical processes

✦ schedules, recounting events in sequence

✦ following rules in sports, scoring during games

✦ number reversals, substitutions.

Diagnosis

Diagnosis can be difficult because dyscalculia often overlaps with other learning difficulties (e.g. *DYSLEXIA*). Assessment should evaluate:

✦ learning **aptitude**/*IQ*

✦ information-processing, particularly visual perception

✦ *LANGUAGE AND SPEECH*

✦ reading **ability** and **achievement**

✦ maths ability and achievement

✦ motor skills

✦ developmental, family and schooling history.

Causes

✦ Visual processing weakness: difficulty visualising numbers and maths situations (e.g. word problems), often with associated weaknesses in spelling and handwriting, but not in reading and creative written language.

✦ Sequencing problems: difficulty organising information, problems remembering specific facts and formulas, often with associated difficulty in **decoding/encoding**, and anything requiring detailed memorisation (e.g. multiplication tables).

Treatment

Dyscalculia is often not diagnosed until a child has been at school for a few years, and by then there are usually knowledge gaps, misunderstandings and a significant lack of confidence (and often not just in maths).

It may be necessary to withdraw the student from Grade-level maths for a period of time (such material is often far too difficult and demoralising). Once a solid skills base is established it will be possible to reintegrate the student into Grade-level lessons.

An individualised maths programme helps teach strategies that enable the student to 'get around' the processing weaknesses that cause the problem.

Strategies

These may include:

✦ going back to basics
✦ allowing manipulation of concrete materials (tens and units blocks, play money, number lines, etc.)
✦ making maths practical (e.g. have the child count how many papers need to be passed out to other students)
✦ using graph paper to help with alignment, setting out, column placements, and so on
✦ using a calculator as a stress-free way to check work
✦ using *LEARNING AIDS*, several of which have been developed specifically for children with the organisational problems typical of dyscalculia.

Further information

The British Dyslexia Association, www.bda-dyslexia.org.uk (accessed 20 September 2005)
National Center for Learning Disabilities, www.ld.org (accessed 20 September 2005)
Department for Education Services, www.dfes.gov.uk (accessed 20 September 2005)

➤➤ Dyslexia: An overview

Dyslexia is a **neurological disorder**, affecting fluent and accurate reading, writing, spelling and, sometimes, number skills.

Common characteristics

In early years, these may include:
+ difficulties dressing, putting shoes on the correct feet; catching, kicking, throwing a ball, hopping, skipping; following simple sequences/patterns; learning nursery rhymes; remembering names of common things (e.g. chair)
+ jumbling sounds (e.g. 'boy tox' for 'toy box')
+ *LANGUAGE AND SPEECH* delay
+ liking stories but showing little interest in letters or words
+ being a bit clumsy, bumping into things
+ seeming not to listen
+ using word substitutions (e.g. 'red engine' for 'fire engine')
+ walking early, but not crawling.

At primary school, these may include:
+ difficulty blending sounds (e.g. s-t-r-a-p), and alphabet letter/sound matching
+ difficulty remembering sequences (e.g. tables, alphabet order)
+ being disorganised, losing things
+ getting 'tongue-tied' using long words (e.g. preliminary)
+ lacking confidence, poor **self-image**
+ leaving letters out of words
+ confusion over left/right, up/down
+ poor level of concentration, listening skills, concept of time, copying (e.g. from board), motor skills (including handwriting, tying laces), reading, reading comprehension, spelling and writing skills
+ problems explaining ideas
+ putting/reading letters, words, numerals the wrong way round (e.g. b/d, on/no)
+ seemingly bright and alert, but failing in key areas
+ slow at written work
+ *INFORMATION PROCESSING DIFFICULTIES*
+ unexplained 'good'/'bad' days
+ using fingers/marks on paper even for simple calculations.

Causes

A specific cause is not yet understood, but what is known is that **genetics** play a part and that neurological **impairment** affects:

✦ phonology: auditory perception of sounds in words and letter sound/symbol matching

✦ information processing speed: keeping up with rapidly changing sound sequences (e.g. in words, multiplication tables), possible 'blurring' of letters/words when reading (caused by an 'after' image of the previous letter)

✦ coordination of auditory perception and processing speed

✦ fluency and organisation of actions (automaticity).

Phonology is currently believed to be the main difficulty, but all the other areas are also significant in the diagnosis of dyslexia and the support and education of dyslexic children.

Diagnosis

Specialist assessment (e.g. *EDUCATIONAL PSYCHOLOGIST*), should include evaluation of:

✦ attention/behaviour (ratings by parents, teacher, etc.)

✦ developmental and family history

✦ first-language skills (the child may be struggling because of culture and language differences)

✦ information processing skills

✦ IQ (verbal, non-verbal)

✦ language and speech

✦ phonological skills (e.g. letter symbols and sounds, rhyme)

✦ physical health

✦ reading, spelling and maths **achievement** levels

✦ spelling and reading single words, words in context and nonsense words

✦ vision and hearing.

Further information

The Dyslexia Institute, www.dyslexia-inst.org.uk (accessed 20 September 2005)

The British Dyslexia Association, www.bda-dyslexia.org.uk (accessed 20 September 2005)

➤➤ Dyslexia: Management

There is no known medical cure for dyslexia; education is currently considered the most positive and successful approach to helping the child with dyslexia. There is some growing evidence that certain natural products, while not cures, can aid concentration and memory.

In most cases, the child with dyslexia is taught in a mainstream setting, with particular support from the classroom teacher. Often there is a need for additional, individual support to help with foundation skills and to develop alternative learning strategies, recuperate lost or misunderstood concepts and gain confidence. There are some schools that offer specialised programmes to help dyslexic students access the school curriculum within a supportive whole school setting.

Strategies

✦ Match expectations to intellectual **ability** as well as learning difficulties.
✦ Try to understand the reasons for a dyslexic child's mistakes and give them a chance to explain the difficulties.
✦ Be slow, quiet and deliberate when giving instructions, allowing time for the meaning of the words to sink in. Consider giving **multi-sensory** instructions (e.g. verbal plus keywords on flashcards).
✦ Where possible, use multi-sensory methods of teaching.
✦ Teach the child how to tackle tasks systematically (demonstrate the technique, give guided practice and help the child build up good organisational skills).
✦ Watch out for signs of tiredness and fatigue – dyslexic children have to try harder than other students, which can be exhausting.
✦ Watch out for signs of falling confidence and **self-esteem**.
✦ Encourage and enable dyslexic children to show their interests, knowledge and skills by using skills they are good at rather than those they struggle with.
✦ Consider the environment: what distractions are there, both at home and at school, when the student needs to be concentrating (e.g. noise, wall posters, window views)? Is there an organised study space with clearly marked and neatly arranged resources so that they can be found easily? Consider a 'study buddy' the dyslexic child can ask to re-explain tasks, clarify instructions. Arrange for a student who can be contacted at home if there is confusion over homework instructions.

➤➤ Dyspraxia

'Dyspraxia is an impairment or immaturity of the organisation of movement. Associated with this there may be problems of language, perception and thought.' (Dyspraxia Foundation)

It is also considered a form of sensory processing disorder (*SENSORY INTEGRATIVE DYSFUNCTION*).

Terminology

✦ Verbal/articulatory Dyspraxia (apraxia) is applied specifically to **impairment**/delay in speech.
✦ Developmental Dyspraxia does not only affect speech/language production, but involves the body's overall movement (motor) system.
✦ Developmental coordination disorder = Developmental Dyspraxia.
✦ Movement describes gross- and fine-motor functions, including **oro-motor** coordination, pencil grasp, posture, and so on.

Developmental Dyspraxia

Research suggests that about 5–6 per cent of children have Developmental (generalised) Dyspraxia. Its severity can vary; some aspects of motor movement can be affected more than others; and boys are more likely to be affected than girls. In the past it has been given various labels (e.g. minimal brain dysfunction, clumsy child syndrome).

Symptoms

Symptoms may include all or a **significant** number of these:

From birth to 3 years:
✦ feeding difficulties (colic, *ALLERGIES*)
✦ lateness in milestones (e.g. sitting, walking, speaking, bowel and bladder control)
✦ obsessive about certain toys, clothing, food
✦ poor speech clarity, poor voice control (loudness, etc.)
✦ *SLEEP PROBLEMS*.

From 3 to 5 years:
✦ 'always' bumping into things, falling over
✦ avoids construction toys, jigsaws
✦ communication difficulties

+ delay in establishing *HAND PREFERENCE*, crossing the **midline**
+ difficulty pedalling a tricycle
+ easily upset, prone to temper tantrums
+ hands flap when running
+ high levels of motor activity (e.g. foot-tapping, hand-clapping)
+ little interest in imaginative play
+ messy eating (difficulty using cutlery, spills drinks)
+ peer interaction difficulties (e.g. isolated, made fun of)
+ poor concentration, poor task completion
+ poor fine-motor skills (e.g. holding a pencil)
+ poor sense of danger
+ overreactive to sensory input (e.g. noise, messy hands)
+ slow response to verbal instructions, questions, and so on; problems with comprehension
+ very excitable, loud/shrill voice.

By 7 years:
+ awkward in PE activities, an 'odd' gait
+ difficulties adapting to school routines
+ difficulties learning foundation school skills (phonics, numbers)
+ dressing difficulties (e.g. slow, managing buttons)
+ immature *DRAWING*, poor *HANDWRITING*, copying
+ obsessive interests.

By 9 years:
+ frequent complaints about not feeling well
+ difficulty with friendships, teasing
+ easily upset, emotional, overexcited
+ failing academically
+ high motor activity levels (leg-jiggling, etc.)
+ language is very literal (e.g. does not 'get' jokes)
+ poor concentration/listening, difficulty remembering more than two instructions at once, multiplication tables, and so on
+ problems using a knife and fork
+ sleep problems
+ slow to start/finish class work
+ unhappy at school.

Causes

It is thought that Dyspraxia is a result of immature or impaired brain-cell development either **in utero** or in early infancy, possibly due to:

✦ in-utero illness, deprivation (e.g. oxygen)

✦ febrile illness (high fever) in the early years

✦ poor diet

✦ **genetic** predisposition – there is often a family history of associated problems (e.g. learning difficulties, *STUTTERING/STAMMERING*).

Under normal circumstances the brain receives sensory messages (from the eyes, touch, smell, etc.) and then sends messages to the muscles, telling them how to react. These messages run along nerve pathways, which, with practice, develop into 'memories' that we can call on without too much conscious planning.

In Dyspraxia, however, it seems that the development of these nerve pathways is interfered with, meaning that they do not get used very often, if at all, and essential movement 'memories' are either not developed or are not very efficient. This is why Dyspraxic children often cannot carry out certain motor actions, use some incorrectly or take so long to organise them that they are not very useful.

Diagnosis

Evaluation should be multi-disciplinary and include assessment by a:

✦ paediatrician

✦ **neurologist**

✦ *EDUCATIONAL PSYCHOLOGIST*

✦ *SPEECH AND LANGUAGE THERAPIST*

✦ *OCCUPATIONAL THERAPIST* and/or *PHYSIOTHERAPIST*

✦ audiologist.

There is no one test for Dyspraxia, but in general there are 5 criteria for diagnosis:

1 Marked impairment in development of motor coordination.

2 The impairment significantly interferes with academic **achievement** or daily living activities.

3 The coordination difficulties are not due to a specific medical condition (e.g. *CEREBRAL PALSY*).

4 It is not a *PERVASIVE DEVELOPMENTAL DISORDER* (*PDD*).

5 Motor difficulties are in excess of those usually associated with developmental delay.

There may be related problems (e.g. *LANGUAGE AND SPEECH* difficulties), as well as co-existing learning and/or behaviour difficulties, e.g. *DYSLEXIA, ATTENTION DEFICIT DISORDERS.*

Treatment and management

Dyspraxic children usually have intellectual **aptitude** within the average range, but can have learning difficulties due to developmental delays, communication problems and/or social and emotional difficulties (e.g. low **self-esteem**).

Typically, a range of practitioners is involved, notably an Occupational Therapist and a Speech and Language Therapist (particularly in the case of Verbal Dyspraxia).

Specialist help is often needed at school to support the child, teachers and parents in school skills and social behaviour.

Dyspraxic children have difficulty responding and learning 'intuitively' and by copying others. New skills (social and/or academic) often need to be very deliberately taught, with lots of guided practice to develop them.

Prognosis

There is no cure for Dyspraxia, but early, appropriate intervention can minimise more extreme difficulties. It is often necessary to maintain structured learning strategies into secondary school, and *PSYCHOTHERAPY* may help adolescents and adults to understand the nature of their Dyspraxia, the problems it creates for them and how best to manage it for themselves.

Further information

Portwood, M., *Developmental Dyspraxia*, 2nd edn, David Fulton Publishers Ltd, London, 1999.
The Dyspraxia Foundation, www.dyspraxiafoundation.org.uk (accessed 20 September 2005)

➤➤ Eating behaviours

The **developmental stages** relating to eating behaviours are as follows:
- sucking – infants obtain milk using a lick/suck action on the nipple or teat
- food manipulation in the mouth – by about 4 months the baby uses the tongue to push food to the back of the mouth and is ready for solids
- holds feeding bottle – about 6 months
- biting and chewing – emerges by about 8 months
- holding a spoon, finger-feeding – about 12 months
- holds a cup independently – about 20 months
- uses spoon, fork – emerging skill from about 3 years onwards
- uses fork and knife – emerging skill by about 5 years.

Influences on eating behaviours

Developmental factors

- Toddlers learning to feed themselves and experimenting with food tend to be messy eaters rather than having an eating problem.
- About age 2, growth starts to slow down and children may eat less than before.
- Between 2 and 4 years, children begin to be assertive (e.g. refusing food, being fussier about certain textures, messiness).

Temperament

- Children who are 'fussier', harder to comfort and not good at routines are often not easy to feed.
- Assertive children often try to 'dictate' what they will/will not eat.

Developmental delay

- Delays in motor skills and coordination can cause problems in the development of eating skills (e.g. sucking, chewing, holding a spoon/knife and fork).

Physical factors

- Poor muscle coordination (e.g. *CEREBRAL PALSY*) or physical inability.
- Chronic illnesses that involve nausea, reflux.
- *CLEFT PALATE* children (food/liquid can escape into the nose).

Early eating experiences

✦ Being tube-fed.

✦ Swallowing difficulties.

Emotional factors

✦ Traumatic events (e.g. birth of a sibling, an accident).

✦ Family stress, causing **anxiety** (e.g. *DIVORCE AND SEPARATION*, arguments).

✦ Neglect, lack of affection.

Parent models

✦ Overanxiety about eating.

✦ Dietary beliefs, religious customs, cultural practices.

✦ Parents' own experiences and anxieties about food (e.g. the child is allowed to eat 'anything' because father grew up under a hated strict food regime).

✦ Family eating behaviours (e.g. family does not sit down to eat).

A good diet

Keeping in mind individual needs, specialists recommend certain daily portions of:

✦ energy-rich, starchy carbohydrates (bread, cereal, pasta, etc.)

✦ fruit and vegetables

✦ dairy, calcium-rich foods (milk drinks/puddings/custards)

✦ protein-rich foods (meat, fish, vegetarian alternatives)

✦ fluids (e.g. milk, water, diluted fruit juices).

In addition:

✦ fatty, sugary foods are not recommended

✦ you should aim for 3 small but regular meals a day, plus 2 healthy snacks

✦ encourage children to try a wide range of foods and textures

✦ avoid added sugar and salt.

Further information

The Children's Food Advisory Service, www.childrensfood.org (accessed 20 September 2005)

➤➤ Eating disorders and obesity

Obesity is an abnormal amount of body fat in proportion to body size. 'Overweight' people have a body-to-fat proportion that is between normal and obese (although still 'technically' obese).

Over the last few years the incidence of being over-weight and obesity in children has increased.

Eating disorders include anorexia, bulimia and binge eating. Eating disorders can be life-threatening problems for females and males. They involve extreme emotions, attitudes and behaviours to do with weight and food, to the extent that the person develops a distorted belief about themselves. Eating disorders follow on from worries about weight and shape, which most often develop in late childhood and through puberty. Causes for weight/shape worries and resultant eating disorders are typically:

✦ biological factors (e.g. **genetics** can determine body shape, tendency to weight gain; puberty)

✦ family factors (e.g. family beliefs and attitudes to food, weight)

✦ sociocultural factors (e.g. class, ethnicity, media and peer influences).

Anorexia nervosa

Anorexia nervosa is characterised by self-starvation and excessive weight loss. Symptoms include:

✦ intense fear of putting on weight or being 'fat'

✦ extreme concern with body weight and shape

✦ feeling 'fat' or over-weight despite dramatic weight loss

✦ refusal to maintain body weight at or above a minimally normal weight for height, body type, age and activity level

✦ changes to body functions (e.g. girls stop menstruating).

Bulimia nervosa

Bulimia nervosa is a secretive cycle of eating large amounts of food (more than most people would eat in one meal) in short periods of time (bingeing), then getting rid of the food and calories by purging (typically self-induced vomiting, improper use of laxatives or overexercising). Symptoms include:

✦ frequent dieting

✦ extreme concern with body weight and shape

✦ repeated episodes of bingeing and purging

✦ 'out of control' eating, eating beyond comfortable fullness.

Binge-eating disorder (compulsive over-eating)

This is uncontrolled, impulsive or continuous eating beyond the point of feeling comfortably full. There is no purging, but other symptoms include:

+ sporadic fasting, repeated dieting
+ feelings of shame or self-hatred after a binge
+ anxiety, *DEPRESSION* and loneliness, which can lead to new episodes of binge eating
+ body weight varying from normal to mild, moderate or severe obesity.

Other eating disorders include combinations of aspects of anorexia, bulimia and/or binge eating. They are not always considered a 'full **syndrome**' **disorder**, but they can still be physically and emotionally dangerous.

All eating disorders require professional help.

Further Information

Eating Disorders Association, UK, www.edauk.com (accessed 20 September 2005)

National Eating Disorders Association, USA, www.edap.org (accessed 20 September 2005)

➤➤ Eating problems

These are different to eating disorders, since, typically, they are not due to psychological distortions about body weight and shape. Eating problems include:

✦ eating the wrong foods, food fads (e.g. liking only mushy food, sweet drinks, crisps)

✦ poor appetite

✦ mealtime behaviours (e.g. not sitting down, spitting out food, tantrums)

✦ overeating

✦ weaning problems

✦ food *ALLERGIES*

✦ **failure to thrive** (grow), a potentially serious eating problem in approximately 2 per cent of young children (most common eating problems do not lead to slow growth, however).

Eating the wrong foods

This can be related to **developmental stage**, *TEMPERAMENT*, neglect, adult models, attitudes, beliefs and family income (foods that cost less are not always as nutritional). Some diets may be nutritionally sufficient for adults, but not for young children unless modified; for example, if a child has a vegetarian diet, care must be taken to ensure an adequate calorie intake, a variety of different plant proteins and appropriate levels of vitamins.

Poor appetite

This can be related to developmental stage (e.g. children often eat less around 2–3 years of age), illness or emotional factors (stress, family arguments, fear).

Mealtime behaviours

Behavioural patterns at mealtimes stem from developmental stage (defiance, asserting independence), temperament (acceptance of routines), adult expectations and models (e.g. is meal-time chaotic, a time for arguments?).

Overeating

This is tied to adult models, anxieties and expectations, the child's emotional state or a medical condition (e.g. a metabolic disorder, some medications). Being over-weight can 'creep up' and, once established, it is often hard to reverse.

Weaning problems

These vary from child to child, since developmental readiness plays a factor, as do parental needs, attitudes and anxieties. The ability to self-feed (e.g. hold the bottle, spoon etc.) plays a part as well.

Food allergies

Allergies to food relate to health and to behaviour. Some children are hypersensitive to certain foods and can have allergic reactions (e.g. hives, nausea). There is evidence to suggest that some children are also susceptible to overactivity/overexcitability after eating particular foods; there is an established link between certain foods and migraine headaches, and some foods can aggravate conditions like *ECZEMA* and *ASTHMA*.

Failure to thrive

A child's failure to thrive is related to medical conditions (e.g. heart, kidney disease), severe feeding difficulties (e.g. swallowing, chewing), poverty and/or factors such as maltreatment (e.g. deliberate withholding of food).

Diagnosing eating problems

Information is obtained from various sources (e.g. parent/carer interview, direct observations, charting eating behaviour, developmental age and stage assessment and medical assessment of weight/height development, medical conditions and allergies).

Parent/carer information can at times be imprecise or deliberately misleading (e.g. in the case of maltreatment) and meal charting is more accurate (although still open to inconsistencies).

Direct observation, while time-consuming, tends to be the most reliable source of information about eating behaviour.

Failure to thrive is usually calculated with a formula that takes genetic tendencies into account (i.e. parents' height and weight), as well as the constancy of the relationship between a child's height and weight from birth onwards. Usually children are expected to maintain that relationship over time (allowing for developmental spurts), and when there is a **significant** change in that relationship then there is greater concern.

Treatment

◆ *BEHAVIOUR MANAGEMENT*, patience and time can often help the child overcome eating problems related to developmental stage, temperament and food fads.

◆ Medical management will be needed in the case of medical conditions, growth disorders and failure to thrive.

◆ Psychological/psychotherapeutic intervention with the child and the parents/carers may be needed to help children with psychosocial disorders (psychological thinking interfered with by social factors).

◆ Other professionals may also be able to help; for example, a *SPEECH AND LANGUAGE THERAPIST* or an *OCCUPATIONAL THERAPIST* can evaluate and provide therapy for **oro-motor** coordination (mouth/tongue/face muscles) or more generalised motor difficulties, and a *SOCIAL WORKER* can intervene in cases of neglect.

➤➤ Eczema

Eczema describes a variety of inflamed skin conditions. Approximately 10 per cent of children experience eczema, but it most often clears with age. Eczema is not contagious.

Causes

Exact causes are unknown, but it seems that in cases of eczema, the inflammatory response of the body's **immune system** is overactive.

Characteristics

Symptoms can vary, but common characteristics include:

+ dry, red, extremely itchy patches on the skin
+ when patches are scratched, the rash appears
+ infant eczema typically occurs on the forehead, cheeks, forearms, legs, scalp and neck
+ in children and adults, it occurs on the face, neck, insides of the elbows, knees and ankles
+ eczema patches can fester and weep or appear scaly, dry and red
+ persistent scratching causes dry, leathery skin.

Itching

Children find it more difficult to understand why they itch, and find it even more difficult not to scratch. Many substances have been identified as itch 'triggers', including:

+ rough or coarse materials making contact with the skin
+ getting too hot, perspiring
+ certain soaps, detergents, disinfectants, contact with juices from fresh fruits, dust mites and animal saliva and fur
+ stress can also sometimes aggravate an existing flare-up.

Diagnosis

A medical doctor and specialist in dermatology should be consulted.

Treatment

+ Prevention/precautions: for example, chart outbreaks and preceding factors to establish triggers and avoid them if possible; moisturise frequently; avoid sudden changes in temperature or humidity, scratchy materials, harsh soaps, detergents; reduce stress.

+ Moisturising creams: ideally, these are applied after bathing to 'lock in' moisture.

+ Cold compresses: to 'cool' itchy skin.

+ **Cortico-steroid** creams/ointments: anti-inflammatory drugs that reduce persistent **inflammation**. Prescription cortico-steroids are more potent than non-prescription forms.

+ Oral cortico-steroids: tablet form medication for severe flare-ups, but side effects (e.g. new episodes) can develop when treatment is discontinued.

+ *ANTIBIOTICS* (creams or oral medication): to treat infected sites.

+ Anti-histamines (tablets, creams): for severe itching (anti-histamines act to stop the production of histamines, which are part of the immune process, but which also cause itching).

+ Tar treatments and phototherapy: both can be effective, although tar can be messy and phototherapy requires special equipment.

+ Immuno-suppressants (e.g. Cyclosporine A): medication which reduces or stops immune system reactions (e.g. inflammation) and thus relieves symptoms; it is more likely to be used when Eczema is resistant to other therapy, since there can be significant side effects.

+ Topical immuno-modulators (TIMs): **steroid**-free drugs that act on skin cells.

Further information

Skin Condition Guide, www.skin-conditions.org (accessed 20 September 2005)

The National Eczema Society, www.eczema.org (accessed 20 September 2005)

➤➤ Educational (School) Psychologists

Educational Psychologists are trained in child and adolescent development and learning, and work in care and education settings as well as in the home. Educational Psychologists who specialise in working with children commonly evaluate and work with children referred because of difficulties with learning, behaviour and development, particularly:

✦ special educational needs and disability (e.g. *ASPERGER'S DISORDER*)

✦ specific behavioural/learning problems and **disorders** (e.g. *ATTENTION DEFICIT DISORDERS*, Oppositional Defiant Disorder)

✦ specific learning difficulties (e.g. *DYSLEXIA*)

✦ social skills (e.g. excessive shyness, aggression).

The Educational Psychologist can work individually with a child, carrying out an assessment, then planning and following through a programme that focuses on the specific skills identified in the evaluation. The Educational Psychologist can also work as a consultant, educating parents and others about the reasons for the child's difficulties, and how the environment might be adapted to support the child and strengthen skills. They demonstrate how to work with the child and how to help the child apply skills, learned in individual therapy sessions, to the mainstream setting.

Evaluation/*TESTING*

Typically, the Educational Psychologist will gather information from parents and from significant others working with the child and will carry out a variety of activities in individual sessions with the child. Evaluation tools usually include:

✦ parent/carer checklists of development and behaviour

✦ observation of the child in the care/education/home setting

✦ **achievement** tests (e.g. pre-literacy skills, reading age)

✦ **standardised** tests of intellectual **aptitude** and **ability** (e.g. WISC-IV, WIAT, Cognitive Assessment Battery)

✦ standardised tests of specific skills (e.g. visual processing).

The Educational Psychologist is able to provide a variety of suggestions and activities that can be used for the child, individually or as part of a group of children (e.g. *BEHAVIOUR MANAGEMENT* strategies), as well as helping to develop an individual education programme. Educational Psychologists can also provide lists of appropriate toys, games and activities for the home.

Further information

www.educational-psychologist.co.uk (a useful links page to other information as well) (accessed 20 September 2005)

➤➤ Epilepsy

Epilepsy is caused by a malfunction in brain-cell chemistry. Brain cells carry messages to and from the brain and within the brain, and inbuilt mechanisms usually ensure that this happens in an orderly way. However, sometimes an unexpected upset in cell chemistry causes the messages to become chaotic, and this disturbed activity triggers a **seizure**.

Diagnosis

This involves developmental history, observations, diagnostic tests (e.g. **brain scans**), assessment of learning or behavioural problems and referral to a specialist (e.g. **neurologist**).

Symptoms

Symptoms may include:
+ frequent, prolonged episodes of rapid blinking or 'staring into space'
+ poor recall of events
+ fainting/collapsing
+ febrile convulsions (muscular spasms, usually caused by a high temperature)
+ breath-holding attacks – an extreme reaction to shock or frustration (the child takes a huge breath as if to scream and holds it until s/he passes out).

Generalised seizure types

Tonic-clonic
Also known as 'grand mal', this is the most common, characterised by:
+ loss of consciousness
+ tonic phase – muscles contract, the body stiffens
+ clonic phase – uncontrollable jerking, there may be a cry as air is forced out of the lungs, lips may go blue (lack of oxygen)
+ no recall of the episode
+ recovery time (often a deep sleep) is needed (from minutes to perhaps hours).

Absence
Also known as 'petit mal', this is more common in children and teenagers, and may look like daydreaming or even go unnoticed. It is characterised by:
+ staring, blinking, looking vague for a few seconds
+ possible body jerks.

Partial seizure types

Simple partial

This occurs in just part of the brain and symptoms vary according to the area affected:

+ twitching, numbness, perspiring, dizziness, nausea, upsets to hearing/vision/smell/taste, déjà vu
+ several seconds' duration
+ the person is fully aware.

Complex partial

This is characterised by strange behaviours (e.g. plucking at clothes, smacking lips, swallowing repeatedly). Some symptoms are similar to simple partial seizures, but there is no awareness of surroundings and no memory of the episode.

Treatment

Treatment may include:

+ avoiding 'triggers' (e.g. flashing lights)
+ anti-epileptic drugs
+ surgery
+ special diet.

In care and education settings, it is important to understand the profile of a child with Epilepsy (e.g. type, medication, what to do in the event of a seizure).

Prognosis

Many children with epilepsy can, with a few sensible precautions, lead normal lives and enjoy doing all the things their friends do (e.g. sports). There are some issues in adolescence that need particular consideration, however (e.g. mixing medication with alcohol).

Most children with epilepsy have normal **intelligence**, although a few may have special learning needs. Difficult-to-control epilepsy, plus other problems (e.g. learning difficulties), is sometimes called 'epilepsy plus'. When the condition is serious, children usually need long-term treatment and support.

Further information

International League Against Epilepsy, www.epilepsy.org (accessed 20 September 2005)

➤➤ Fever

Fever occurs when the body's 'thermostat' (located in the brain) raises the body temperature above its normal level (about 37° Celsius/98.5° Fahrenheit). Body temperature can fluctuate during the day, according to weather and activity level. It can also be a symptom of:

✦ *INFECTIONS*: fever helps the body fight infections by stimulating the **immune system**.

✦ Overdressing: infants, especially newborns, may get fevers if they are overdressed or if the weather is very hot, because at such a young age the body temperature control system is not yet efficient.

✦ Immunisations: babies and children sometimes get a low-grade fever after a vaccination.

✦ Teething: this may cause a slight rise in body temperature, but rarely higher than 37.8°C (100°F).

Temperature can go up and down, causing shivering and sweats. Shivering helps the body to create additional heat as the body's temperature begins to rise, and then, as the temperature starts to drop, the child sweats to help the body release extra heat. Rapid breathing and a fast heartbeat can also occur, and these are symptoms that should be checked by a doctor.

When is a temperature too high?

✦ 37.5°C/99.5°F measured orally

✦ 37.2°C/99°F measured under the arm

✦ 38°C/100.4°F measured rectally.

But a high fever does not always indicate serious illness. A simple cold can sometimes cause a high fever, while a serious infection can cause an abnormally low body temperature, especially in young infants.

Thermometers

✦ Digital thermometers usually provide the quickest, most accurate readings and can be used for taking oral, underarm and rectal temperatures.

✦ Electronic ear thermometers are not advised for infants under 3 months.

✦ Plastic strip thermometers (small plastic strips to press against the child's forehead) can indicate a fever, but are not an exact measurement.

◆ Pacifier (dummy) thermometers require the child to keep the pacifier in the mouth for several minutes without moving, which is quite impractical for most babies and toddlers, and these are not advised for infants under 3 months.

◆ Glass mercury thermometers are no longer in extensive use (due to fear of mercury poisoning, glass breaking, etc.).

Further information

General health website, www.kidshealth.org (accessed 20 September 2005)

➤➤ Gifted (able and talented) children: An overview

This topic abounds with debate and definitions. For example, 'gifted' can describe the top 5 per cent of a school population in academic subjects; 'talented' the top 5 per cent in other subjects; and 'more able' the top 30 per cent. (However, only those with an IQ score in the top 2 per cent of the population would be eligible for membership of MENSA, a worldwide organisation for people with very high scores in an **IQ test**).

Definitions and terminology aside, the evidence indicates fairly consistently that giftedness:

+ does not always mean a high IQ score
+ does not always mean that the child performs outstanding feats for age and stage
+ does not necessarily mean business or career success in adult life
+ does not mean that children do not share in **developmental stages** and phases (e.g. teenage rebellion)
+ as measured in children, is different to that in adults
+ can be general or specific
+ can be the same as 'very able' or 'talented'
+ can be an advantage or a disadvantage
+ can coexist with a learning difficulty
+ cannot be measured by one test
+ is not always the same as academic success.

Factors in giftedness

Intelligence

As measured on a **standardised** test, **intelligence** is **aptitude** for learning. A high IQ (intelligence measure) is associated with faster learning of more difficult concepts, greater creative and problem-solving abilities and deeper insight into complex issues; but this does not mean that all these traits will be seen in all children with a high IQ. In addition, while most highly successful people in any field are in the top 5–20 per cent of IQ scores, not all of them are. Therefore, identifying giftedness means looking beyond intelligence as measured by IQ scores.

Developmental differences

Typically, some children go forward more rapidly than others in all or some areas, then 'plateau', then advance again. Others move on steadily across all areas. Still others develop rapidly in some or all areas and continue to do so, and they stand out from their peers. At this point they may feel different, become bored by activities, or be 'clever' at some things but average or delayed in others (e.g. able to solve complex maths relative to age but unable to tie shoelaces).

Personality traits

Studies of gifted, talented and highly successful people show certain shared characteristics (e.g. tenacity, initiative, skills in overcoming setbacks, motivation, positive **self-esteem** and independence).

Environmental influences

Influences include people the child comes into contact with (e.g. parents, teachers), access to resources (e.g. libraries, computers, gifted programmes in school) and where the child lives (e.g. city, country, developed country, less developed country).

Further information

British MENSA, www.mensa.org.uk (accessed 20 September 2005)

The Support Society for Children of High Intelligence, www.chi-charity.org.uk (accessed 20 September 2005)

The National Literacy Trust, www.literacytrust.org.uk (search term: gifted children) (accessed 20 September 2005)

➤➤ Gifted children: Identification

Methods of identification tends to vary with age and setting. The following provide some examples:

✦ Parents, friends, health visitors or doctors may notice a young child (0–4 years) developing skills far more quickly than similarly aged children.

✦ Playgroup and reception-class teachers may notice a child can do far more than usual for their age (2–5 years).

✦ Primary and secondary teachers may note easy task completion and a demand for challenge (4 years +).

✦ Children may achieve significantly high scores (using the idea of the top 2 per cent of the population) on standardised tests of:

   a general intellectual **ability** and aptitude (above IQ 130)

   b specific **achievement** (e.g. reading, maths, science)

   c specific ability and aptitude

   d creative and productive thinking

   e leadership ability

   f talent in the visual/performing arts

   g psycho-motor ability (e.g. mechanical skills).

✦ Observations of:

   a a high degree of general knowledge, wide vocabulary/word knowledge, strong memory and good **abstract** reasoning

   b consistently high marks on various academic tests

   c positive **self-image**, very good concentration, willingness to try new ideas, looks at things from a different point of view

   d high degree of responsibility, cooperation, organisation skills

   e unusually good at solving visual problems (e.g. complex jigsaws).

There seems to be agreement that identifying potential for giftedness is more likely to be reliable than identifying giftedness itself, and that giftedness is not just about school success or high IQ, but about creativity, personality traits and specific skills as well.

Gifted children and learning difficulties

✦ 5–10 per cent of gifted children may also have a learning difficulty (e.g. sensory or physical **impairment**, specific learning difficulty). Conversely, approximately 2–5 per cent of children with a difficulty may also be gifted.

✦ Gifted children with learning difficulties may have some below-average skills but be gifted in others. This can lead to uneven performance and the 'giftedness' may go unnoticed or may be assumed across the board.

✦ Children with a learning difficulty often have low **self-esteem**, a lack of confidence, ineffective learning strategies and poor attention and task-completion skills, and, as a result, never get the chance to show some of the characteristics that might otherwise identify giftedness.

Identification of these children is interfered with by the stereotype of gifted children as happy, industrious and academically successful, and by the tendency to evaluate a child for either giftedness *or* disability, but not both.

It would seem that in order to detect potential and nurture it, child care and education settings need to pay attention to managing the environment, developing personality traits, encouraging curiosity and interests, and making different styles of working and learning available for all children.

Further information

Gifted and Talented World, www.gtworld.org (accessed 20 September 2005)
New South Wales Association for Gifted and Talented Children, Inc, www.nswagtc.org.au (accessed 20 September 2005)

➤➤ Hand preference

This is the reliable and consistent use of either the right or the left hand and arm.

Theories about hand preference

+ Psychological/environmental: hand preference is learned by copying adults and through environmental pressure to use one hand over another.
+ **Genetic** (inherited): there is a 'right-hand predisposition' (but if this is not inherited then environment will play a stronger role in deciding handedness).
+ Pathology (health of the brain): this theory holds that we were all meant to be right-handed and that left-handedness is due to brain injury. (There is evidence that a *small* percentage of left-handers were meant to be right-handed, but that brain trauma interfered with right-hand dominance and left-hand dominance was developed to compensate.)

Left-handedness

Left-handedness occurs in about 10 per cent of the population and there are varying degrees of left-handedness (e.g. some children write with their left hand but use their right for other tasks).

Left- and right-handed children without learning problems show no pattern of differences in overall **intelligence**, language **impairment**s and motor skills. Delay in establishing a dominant hand is more likely to be associated with learning and motor problems than simply being right- or left-handed.

Left-handedness is more common in children with *EPILEPSY*, **intellectual impairment** and *AUTISM*, but the **disorder**s are due to damage to the left side of the brain (interfering with right-hand dominance), not due to being right- or left-handed.

Left-handedness in itself is rarely a problem, but being a minority in a world largely set up for right-handers can be.

Some typical 'leftie' problems

+ Awkward, tiring writing style, poor writing posture, smudging writing as they go.
+ Bumping into the right-hander sitting alongside.
+ Using computers with a right-hand mouse and click mechanism.
+ Left-handed children copying some actions from right-handers (and vice versa) can result in considerable confusion.

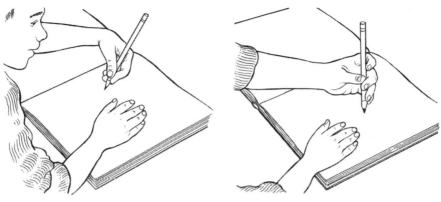

Fig 9 ▲ Hook grasp   **Fig 10 ▲** Ulnar grasp

✦ Pens, scissors, and so on, are often 'automatically' handed to the child's right or placed on their right.

✦ Right-handed flip tables on lecture-hall chairs.

✦ Slower writing speed and development of inefficient pen grasps and writing styles (e.g. the 'hook' pencil grasp or the ulnar grasp, see figures 9 and 10).

Some solutions

✦ Find someone who is left-handed to demonstrate activities (e.g. doing up buttons).

✦ Group left-handed children together when modelling early visual-motor skills (e.g. writing, cutting).

✦ Seat the left-hander to the left of the table and away from a wall on their left.

✦ Show left-handed children how to position pages (reading and writing) in front of them. They should make a triangle on the table with their arms forming two sides of the triangle and their hands clasped together to make the top (apex) of the triangle. The page is placed inside this triangle, lined up with the left arm and then moved so that the page is to the left of the child's **midline** (see figure 11).

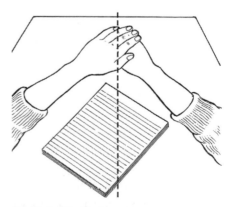

Fig 11 ▲ Positioning paper

✦ Keep **developmental stages** in mind; for example, a 'fist' grasp is typical of 3- and even 4-year-olds experimenting with drawing, scribbling, and so on.

✦ Left-handers need to hold their writing tool 2–3 cm from the tip.

✦ Softer lead pencils are recommended for left-handers.

✦ Provide left-handed equipment (e.g. scissors, musical instruments, button boards, pencil grips, rulers – and colour code them so they are easily identifiable).

✦ Provide plenty of left-to-right practice activities (e.g. tracing, tracking, dot-to-dots, patterns, 'writing' on the board, easels, slanted surfaces).

Further information

Anything Left-handed, www.anythingleft-handed.co.uk (accessed 20 September 2005)

➤➤ Handwriting

Handwriting (holding a pencil/pen and forming letters and numbers) is an academic skill that allows children to express their thoughts and feelings and communicate their knowledge. Handwriting requires multiple skills, including vision, memory, muscle tone and posture.

Readiness for writing

Poor handwriting and an awkward pencil grasp are often the result of children starting to write before they are developmentally ready, and there are signs that indicate this; for example:

✦ Can the child cross the **midline**?

✦ Can the child differentiate fingers (e.g. play 'Incy Wincy Spider' and other finger games and songs)?

✦ Can the child draw the different shapes and lines that make up English letter symbols (e.g. a circle, vertical line starting from the top, horizontal line and diagonal line)?

✦ Can the child identify shapes, symbols, letters and numbers as the same or different (visual and auditory discrimination)?

✦ Can the child identify directional differences in pictures (e.g. find the cup with the handle on the other side from a row of 4; find the chair that is upside down)?

✦ Can the child identify items missing from a picture (initially very obvious omissions, such as the legs on the elephant, to ever finer detail such as the window on the house, the whiskers on the cat)?

✦ Can the child recognise and say the letters being taught (e.g. find the letter 'b' from other alphabet letters; say the sound of the letter 'b' as in 'bat')?

✦ Does the child have bilateral skills (i.e. holding the paper with one hand while colouring/writing with the other)?

✦ Does the child have fairly good control of the pencil (a dynamic grasp i.e. not a lot of shifting of the hand or fingers when changing position) and maintain fairly consistent use of one hand (lateral dominance, *HAND PREFERENCE*)?

✦ Does the child understand the words used when being taught to write (e.g. middle, up, down, around, bottom, top)?

✦ Is the child interested in writing letters, numbers, words, and writing things to show you (even if they are indecipherable)?

✦ When the child holds a pencil, does it look awkward?

Development of hand control

These stages tend to overlap, with the child often in the final stages of one while showing signs of the next:

✦ Scribbling: this is making marks on paper, ideally using different utensils (e.g. finger painting, crayons, pencils, paintbrushes).

✦ Emerging control: still 'scribbling', but a few recognisable shapes appearing.

✦ Copying: basic to correct letter formation.

✦ Independent hand control (not necessarily with a dominant hand): appears around 5 years of age.

Readiness strategies

✦ Accommodate children who have established right- or left-hand preference, as well as those who are still experimenting (e.g. do not sit emerging writers adjacent to each other, but around a desk, with plenty of elbow room).

✦ Allow children to play randomly with letter and number shapes.

✦ Encourage the development of a tripod grasp (see figure 12) through fine-motor activities (e.g. paper tearing, pasting, finger painting, manipulating small objects) and demonstrating it for children.

✦ Ensure tables and chairs are the right height. Children's feet should be comfortably on the floor with arms resting easily on the desk top (not reaching up to the table or the body leaning down over the table).

✦ Let the child choose which hand to use for writing (children often start out using both hands interchangeably, but then develop lateral dominance and eye-hand preference).

✦ Make sure children are sitting comfortably when they are working on pencil-and-paper tasks (preferably at a desk or table), and that they are relaxed. In some instances, lying on the floor or working on a slanted surface can help develop muscle tone and strength, and may be recommended for some children with motor difficulties (e.g. *DYSPRAXIA*).

✦ Provide a variety of **multi-sensory** activities; for example, cutting and sticking pictures; dough/plasticine play; simple

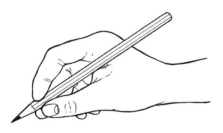

Fig 12 ▲ Tripod grasp

jigsaw puzzle (moving from large to smaller pieces); colouring small and large pictures using different tools; tracing pictures; simple dot-to-dot pictures; playing with wooden bricks or building blocks; copying, tracing, colouring letters and simple words.

Fig 13 ▲ Right-hander position and posture

✦ Allow a wide range of tools to experiment with (e.g. fingers, pencils, pens, chalk, crayons, different-sized paintbrushes).

✦ Provide different surfaces to experiment with and learn how to manipulate (e.g. rough, smooth, large, small, fabric, paper).

✦ Provide opportunities for finger plays and action songs (e.g. I Have 10 Little Fingers, Incy Wincy Spider).

Fig 14 ▲ Left-hander position and posture

✦ Provide plenty of discrimination activities (e.g. inset shape puzzles, matching games, colour the picture that is different, 'what's missing?').

✦ Work towards a good writing position and posture for the child, with appropriate furniture, materials, development activities and using your own writing (grasp and position) as a model as well.

Further information

LDOnLine, www.ldonline.org (accessed 20 September 2005)

➤➤ Handwriting problems: Dysgraphia

Dysgraphia is the inability to write properly, despite being given adequate time and help.

Symptoms

The following symptoms are of concern when they exist beyond developmental expectations and cannot be explained by any other difficulty or disability:

✦ irregular letter sizes, shapes, slants and spaces between words
✦ mixture of upper/lower case or print/cursive letters
✦ poor layout (e.g. does not follow margins)
✦ poor motor control, posture
✦ poor pen grip (too tight, too close to tip, too loose)
✦ poor/bizarre spelling, letter reversals
✦ slow writing and copying, quick to tire
✦ unfinished letters
✦ writing is untidy and difficult to read
✦ written quality very poor relative to spoken language skills.

Causes

Causes may include:

✦ delayed development of eye/hand dominance (*LATERALITY*)
✦ delayed/poor motor skills, possibly related to a specific **disorder** (e.g. *DYSPRAXIA*)
✦ family history of similar difficulties (e.g. *DYSLEXIA*)
✦ poor pen grasp, poor posture
✦ poor visual memory (e.g. of what letters/words/numbers, etc. look like)
✦ poor visual processing of letters and words
✦ poor visual-motor transfer (transferring what is seen into written form).

Diagnosis

Overall development should be evaluated, particularly by an *EDUCATIONAL PSYCHOLOGIST* and an *OCCUPATIONAL THERAPIST*, with input from other specialists as appropriate (e.g. **neurologist**).

Treatment/strategies

Specialist input

This might include a learning specialist or an Occupational Therapist.

Sample activities

✦ Talk through motor sequences (e.g. 'b' is 'big stick down, circle away from my body').

✦ Threading coloured beads.

✦ Tracing, colouring, finger painting, dot-to-dot pictures/lines/patterns/ shapes, left/right tracing activities.

✦ Dough play, using biscuit cutters, swimming, activities that develop body image (e.g. t'ai chi, judo).

✦ Writing in the air with a range of movements (e.g. big arm movements, whole hand, fingers) to improve motor memory of shapes, letters, numbers.

Special aids/equipment

✦ Encourage proper grip, posture and paper positioning (reinforce early to prevent 'bad' habits that are hard to change).

✦ Experiment to find the pens/pencils that are most comfortable.

✦ Use foam pencil grips, and so on, which help to hold the pencil correctly.

✦ Use paper with raised lines (a sensory guide to help stay within the lines).

✦ Let children follow pre-formed letter shapes with their fingers.

✦ Make sloping boards available.

✦ Use templates, which help to keep paper in the right place/at the right angle.

✦ Use word-processing aids.

Different expectations

✦ Allow use of print or cursive – whichever is more comfortable.

✦ Modify rate and amount of written work to be produced.

✦ Provide different equipment (e.g. word processor, lined paper, page guides, pen type).

✦ Simplify written tasks.

✦ Student completes written tasks in small steps instead of all at once.

Further information

Handwriting Help for Kids, www.handwritinghelpforkids.com (accessed 20 September 2005)

Benefits Now, www.benefitsnowshop.co uk (accessed 20 September 2005)

➤➤ Hearing: How we hear

The human ear is made up of the external ear, the middle ear, the inner ear and parts of the brain.

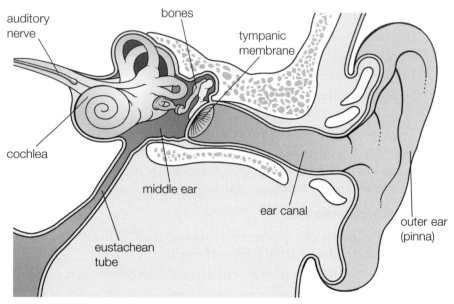

Fig 15 ▲ The ear

The external ear (pinna and ear canal)

The pinna is the shell-like, visible part of the ear. Its folds help us hear by reducing distracting background noise.

The ear canal is a narrow, twisting tube about 2.5 cm long, leading in from the pinna. Glands in this canal produce wax, which helps to maintain humidity and prevent dust and/or objects from going deeper. Any wax build-up should be removed by an audiologist or a physician if it does not come out naturally. Using a cotton-tip bud or anything else can push the wax deeper into the canal and can also harm the canal walls (which are very delicate).

The middle ear (tympanic membrane and ossicles/bones)

The middle ear is an air-filled space that contains the tympanic membrane (eardrum) and a chain of three tiny bones. Sounds travel down the ear canal and strike the tympanic membrane, and the resulting vibrations are transferred to the chain of bones, which also vibrate. These vibrations then transfer the sound they are carrying to the window of the inner ear.

In addition, a tube (Eustachian tube) runs between the throat and the middle ear, allowing fresh air to fill the middle ear as needed. For example, high altitudes cause an increase in air pressure outside the ear and the tympanic membrane bends as a result. At this point, the Eustachian tube opens and allows air in to balance the pressure, and the tympanic membrane unbends and 'pops' back to its original position (the popping sensation experienced when flying on an aeroplane). If the Eustachian tube becomes blocked by infection, fluid may form in the middle ear space (**otitis media**).

The inner ear (vestibular and cochlea)

The cochlea is the snail-shaped part of the inner ear, and it is here that 'hearing' really starts to happen. The cochlea is filled with fluid and the vibrations from the middle ear create pressure waves in the fluid. These waves travel down the canal, bending small hair-type cells, and these, in turn, send nerve impulses to the brain where they are perceived as sound.

The vestibular portion of the inner ear helps to maintain balance.

Further information

Audiology Awareness Campaign, www.audiologyawareness.com (accessed 20 September 2005)

➤➤ Hearing: Types of hearing loss

Hearing ability can range from normal to profound loss. Ranges for children vary according to age and **developmental stage** and differ from adult ranges, since children tend not to respond as reliably as adults. The typical ranges for adults are:

✦ −10 dB to 25 dB = normal range

✦ 26 dB to 40 dB = mild loss

✦ 41 dB to 55 dB = moderate loss

✦ 56 dB to 70 dB = moderately severe loss

✦ 71 dB to 90 dB = severe loss

✦ over 90 dB = profound loss

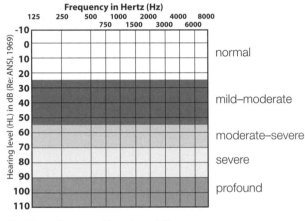

Fig 16 ▲ Range of hearing ability

Hearing loss can develop at any age and may be caused by many different factors. Most hearing losses can be categorised as sensori-neural, conductive or mixed (a combination of sensori-neural and conductive). It is important to understand the basic anatomy of the ear and hearing mechanisms before reading about the actual types of hearing loss.

Sensori-neural hearing loss

Sensori-neural hearing losses occur when the inner ear becomes damaged. About 90 per cent of all people with a hearing **impairment** are in this category. It is sometimes referred to as 'nerve deafness', but this is not a good description because the damage usually occurs within the inner ear and not to the hearing nerve.

Common causes of sensori-neural hearing loss are ageing and exposure to loud noises. This type of hearing loss is not usually treatable, medically or surgically, but many people find that wearing a hearing aid is of significant benefit.

Conductive hearing loss

Conductive hearing loss occurs when either the external ear or the middle ear fails to work properly. Sounds are 'blocked' and are not carried all the way to the inner ear. Conductive hearing loss can often be treated with either medicine or surgery.

Common causes of conductive hearing loss are fluid build-up in the middle ear or a blockage of wax in the ear canal. Children are more likely to have a conductive hearing loss than a sensori-neural hearing loss.

Mixed hearing loss

Mixed hearing loss is simply a combination of the above two types of hearing loss; for example, when a person with a permanent sensori-neural hearing loss also develops a temporary conductive hearing loss.

➤➤ Hearing: Reading an audiogram

An audiogram is a chart of hearing ability. There is usually a standard layout and set of symbols to show frequency and decibels (pitch and loudness).

✦ The frequency scale is read across the top. Frequencies are low on the left (125 or 250 Hz), and gradually increase on the right (8000 Hz).

✦ The decibel scale goes from top to bottom, very soft (–10 or 0 dB) to very loud (110 dB).

✦ 0 dB is the threshold (this is not 'no sound', but the softest sound that a person with normal hearing would hear at least 50 per cent of the time). Normal conversational speech is about 45 dB.

✦ Most audiograms use a standard set of symbols. For air-conduction tests, 'O' indicates the right-ear thresholds and 'X' indicates left-ear thresholds. For bone-conduction tests, a '<' symbol indicates right-ear thresholds and '>' indicates the left.

Sample audiograms

The sample audiograms below show left-ear results for a person with normal hearing, followed by examples for mixed, conductive and sensori-neural loss.

The white area represents the sounds that the person would not hear (softer than thresholds), and the grey area indicates all the sounds that the person would hear (louder than thresholds).

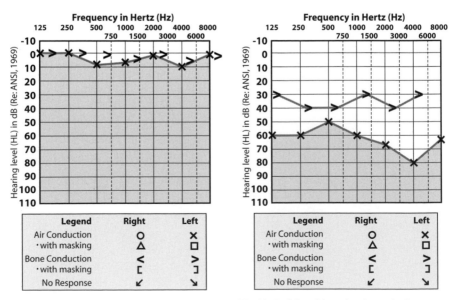

Fig 17 ▲ Normal hearing: Left ear

Fig 18 ▲ Mixed hearing loss: Left ear

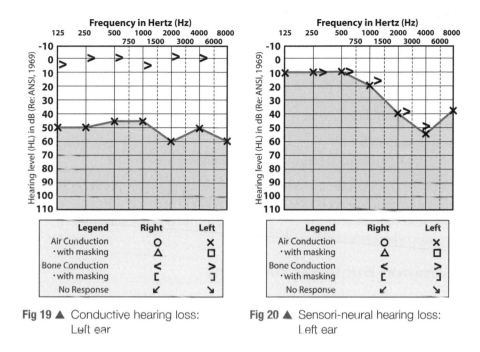

Fig 19 ▲ Conductive hearing loss:
Left ear

Fig 20 ▲ Sensori-neural hearing loss:
Left ear

Further information

Hear It, www.hear-it.org (accessed 20 September 2005)

➤➤ Infections: Bacterial

Infections are invasions of the body that are potentially harmful and that trigger the body's **immune system**. This begins with the production of white blood cells (e.g. lymphocytes), which release chemicals that attack and destroy the 'invaders', and also produce *FEVER*, **inflammation** and the other signs typical of an infection.

Bacteria are single cells that can multiply by themselves. Bacteria exist inside and outside our bodies; some are 'good' and some are harmful.

ANTIBIOTICS can be effective against bacterial infections (unlike most viral infections: see *INFECTIONS: VIRAL*), and some bacterial infections can be prevented with immunisation (e.g. diphtheria, meningitis, pneumonia, pertussis/whooping cough, tetanus).

Common bacterial infections

✦ 'Strep' throat is a painful inflammation of the throat caused by Group A Streptococci (type of bacteria that produces excessive mucus/liquid). There is often a fever above 38.3°C, with chills, body aches and loss of appetite. Some cases result in Scarlet Fever.

✦ *MIDDLE EAR INFECTIONS* (**otitis media**) are infections of the middle ear caused by bacteria or viruses entering the Eustachian tube. The middle ear fills with fluid (pus), building up pressure and causing pain. The eardrum cannot vibrate and hearing is often temporarily affected. When ear infections reoccur, drainage tubes may be inserted (tympanostomy, grommets) to ventilate the area behind the eardrum and drain excess fluid away. Research indicates that recurrent periods of hearing loss caused by ear infections can affect speech development and learning.

✦ Impetigo is a skin infection that usually affects pre-school and school-age children, especially in the summer. A child is more likely to develop impetigo if the skin has already been irritated (e.g. by *ECZEMA*, insect bites, a skin allergy). Impetigo is highly contagious, spreading by contact with infected skin, clothing, and so on. It can be accompanied by Scarlet Fever.

✦ Scarlet Fever is a skin rash that spreads from the neck and face to the rest of the body and is accompanied by a high fever and swollen glands. The rash usually disappears after 5 or 6 days, after which the skin often peels.

✦ Sinusitis is a bacterial infection in the sinus spaces in the face (it can also
be part of a viral infection, such as a cold). It can be acute (single
episode, short duration), sub-acute (1–4 months) or chronic (more than
4 months). It can be confused with *ALLERGIES*. Symptoms include
stuffy nose, facial pain/swelling, headaches, snoring and poor sleep.

Further information

Information on various aspects of children's health, www.kidshealth.com (accessed 20 September 2005)

The Merck Manual of Medical Information, www.merck.com/mmhe/index.html (use alphabetical search) (accessed 20 September 2005)

➤➤ Infections: Viral

A virus is a small organism that cannot multiply by itself (unlike bacteria). It has to invade a living cell to reproduce itself (clone). These clones then infect other cells, reproduce, and so on. Viruses usually only infect one particular type of cell (e.g. cold viruses infect cells in the upper respiratory system, gastric viruses infect cells in the gastric system).

When a virus enters a cell, the body's **immune system** is triggered. This begins with the production of white blood cells (lymphocytes), which can attack and destroy a virus. They can also remember it should it return. This means that should the virus invade again, the immune system can respond more quickly and effectively – this is immunity. Immunity can also come from a **vaccine**.

Common viral infections

✦ Adenoviruses infect the respiratory tract, the eyes, the intestines and the urinary tract, and are highly contagious. Common adenoviruses include:

  a   upper and lower respiratory tract infections

  b   gastroenteritis (an **inflammation** of the stomach and the small and large intestines)

  c   urinary tract infections

  d   eye infections (e.g. conjunctivitis, 'pink eye')

  e   combinations (e.g. pharyngo-conjunctival fever, affecting both the eye and respiratory tract).

Adenoviral infections affect infants and young children much more frequently than adults. Since there are many different types of adenoviruses, repeated infections can occur. Once a child is exposed to an adenovirus, symptoms can develop from 2 days to 2 weeks later. In small children, adenoviruses also commonly cause croup and inflammation of the windpipe (laryngitis) or airways deeper inside the lungs (e.g. bronchitis).

✦ Chicken Pox (varicella) causes a red, itchy skin rash that usually appears first on the abdomen or back and face, and then spreads to almost everywhere else on the body. The rash spots develop into thin-walled blisters filled with fluid, and when the blister breaks, the sores crust over, form scabs and heal. There may be fever, stomach pain or nausea a day or two before the rash appears, and Chicken Pox blisters appear in bouts over 2–4 days. Some children have only a few blisters, whereas others have hundreds. Symptoms may last for a few days, and fever usually stays in the range of 37.7–38.8°C (100–102°F). Younger children often have milder symptoms and fewer blisters than older children or adults. Chicken Pox can be more extensive or severe in children with a skin **disorder** (e.g. *ECZEMA*).

✦ Influenza (the 'flu) infects the respiratory tract. Children tend to get it more often than adults, and most cases occur between early winter and early spring. The 'flu and the common cold are often confused, but flu symptoms tend to develop more quickly and are usually more severe than the typical sneezing and stuffiness of a cold. Flu symptoms include: *FEVER*, chills/shivering, headache, muscle aches, dizziness, loss of appetite, tiredness, cough, sore throat, runny nose, nausea or vomiting, weakness, **ear infection**, diarrhoea. Symptoms are usually gone within a week or two, although a cough and weakness may linger. It is important to treat the 'flu seriously, because it can lead to pneumonia and other complications.

✦ Measles attacks the respiratory system. Symptoms include irritability, runny nose, eyes that are red and sensitive to light, a hacking cough, and a fever (as high as 105°F/40.6°C), peaking when the well-known rash appears. Small, red spots with blue-white centres (Koplick's spots) usually appear in the mouth 1–2 days before the rash. Total time for the rash, from beginning to end, head to toe, is usually about 6 days. Infants are generally protected for 6–8 months after birth, because immunity is passed on from the mother, and older children are usually **immunised** against Measles with a vaccine.

✦ Mumps usually spreads through saliva and can infect many parts of the body, especially the salivary glands between the ear and jaw. Mumps may start with a fever of up to 39.4°C/103°F, as well as a headache and loss of appetite. The glands usually become increasingly swollen and painful over a period of 1–3 days. Most cases of Mumps are in children aged 5–14 years, and are uncommon in children under 12 months. After a case of Mumps it is very unusual to have a second bout, because one attack almost always gives lifelong immunity.

➤➤ Information processing difficulties

In order to learn, we take in information, send it to various parts of the brain, make sense of it, adjust what we already know to make room for anything new, store it for later use or discard it as unimportant. All our senses are involved, but hearing (auditory) and vision (visual) are primary.

Auditory processing difficulty

This is commonly categorised as:

✦ auditory perceptual: interpreting/using what is heard, by reasoning, thinking, and so on

✦ auditory discrimination: recognising sounds as same/different

✦ auditory-sequential: recognising the order of sounds, repeating/reordering them

✦ auditory memory: remembering auditory detail for immediate use or for recall at a later date.

Symptoms

These may include:

✦ difficulty following verbal instructions, getting started on tasks

✦ difficulty retelling sequences of events (e.g. a story)

✦ dreamy, vague, needs instructions repeated

✦ poor attention/concentration for verbal information

✦ poor spelling, especially phonetic words; sounds are omitted, misheard, and so on

✦ slow, hesitant reading.

Diagnosis

This should involve:

✦ gathering a family history of *HEARING* loss, *ALLERGIES*, poor reading/spelling, learning difficulties (e.g. *DYSLEXIA, ATTENTION DEFICIT DISORDERS (ADD)*)

✦ information about the child's developmental and health history (e.g. chronic **ear infections**, allergies)

✦ an ear, nose and throat evaluation: check of nasal passages, ear passages, Eustachian tube, sinuses, *ADENOIDS* and *TONSILS*, hearing (air and bone conduction, background noise)

✦ an assessment of auditory and visual processing skills and **aptitude**.

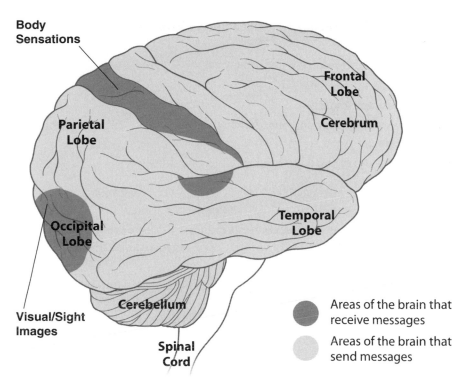

Fig 21 ▲ Diagram of brain areas

Visual processing difficulty

This is commonly categorised as:

✦ visual perception: interpreting/using what is seen
✦ visual discrimination: recognising visual stimuli (pictures, shapes, numerals) as same/different
✦ visual-sequential: ordering visual images, repeating or reordering them
✦ visual memory: remembering visual detail for immediate use or for recall at a later date
✦ visual-motor: integration of vision and muscle movements (e.g. handwriting, catching).

Symptoms

These may include:

✦ difficulty telling time, reading clocks, graphs, maps
✦ letter, number and word reversals, omissions and/or letter substitutions when reading and spelling
✦ physical awkwardness, clumsiness, poor at sports, loses belongings

✦ poor attention/concentration when information is highly visual (e.g. maps, graphs)
✦ poor comprehension of written material
✦ poor spelling
✦ slow, hesitant reading
✦ untidy writing, poor copying/drawing skills, poor presentation/layout on the page
✦ working close to the page/head tilted to one side.

Diagnosis

This should involve:

✦ family history (e.g. glasses, colour blindness, *VISION* problems, poor reading and spelling, untidy writing, poor organisational skills, learning difficulties such as dyslexia)
✦ gathering information about the child's developmental and health history (e.g. allergies, sore/infected eyes)
✦ an ophthalmologist's assessment (e.g. short/long sight, colour blindness, disease, lazy eye, *IRLEN SYNDROME*)
✦ assessment of auditory and visual processing skills and aptitude.

➤➤ Irlen Syndrome (Meares-Irlen/Scotopic sensitivity syndrome)

This is a profile of problems experienced by some people when they are reading (and possibly writing, spelling and doing maths). Problems include:

+ overlapping of letters, words and numbers
+ eye strain and fatigue while reading (especially under fluorescent lights)
+ poor reading comprehension (because focusing takes effort and concentration)
+ short attention span for visual tasks (caused by fatigue, distortions, poor comprehension).

Olive Meares, and later Helen Irlen, described this profile of problems. Helen Irlen went on to show the positive effects of coloured backgrounds and coloured plastic overlays. The **syndrome** is not yet widely recognised, but there is increasing evidence to support its existence. It is thought to be a visual perceptual (information processing) problem rather than a *VISION* problem.

Irlen Syndrome can occur in addition to the need for corrective prescription lenses (glasses), and it is thought likely to be more serious for children, since visual perceptual problems can interfere significantly with school learning and academic success.

Symptoms

These include:

+ eye rubbing
+ excessive blinking
+ poor concentration
+ poor reading
+ poor reading comprehension
+ difficulty keeping place
+ complaints about glare from page, blurring of print
+ complaints of headaches, sore eyes, stomach aches, being tired or sleepy, discomfort.

Distortions described by Irlen Syndrome

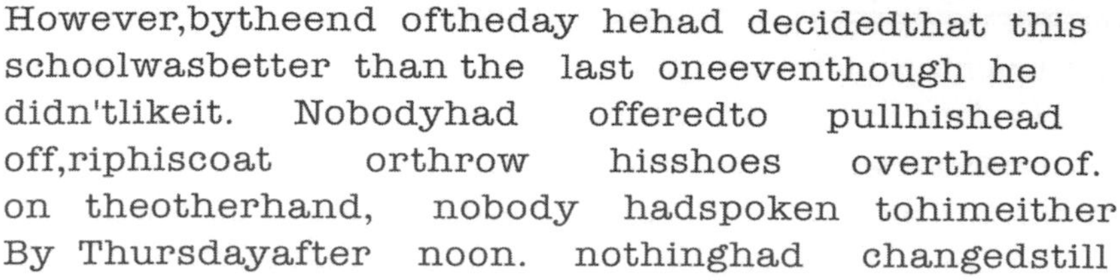

However,bytheend oftheday hehad decidedthat this schoolwasbetter than the last oneeventhough he didn'tlikeit. Nobodyhad offeredto pullhishead off,riphiscoat orthrow hisshoes overtheroof. on theotherhand, nobody hadspoken tohimeither By Thursdayafter noon. nothinghad changedstill

Fig 22 ▲ Rivers

PROMISES PROMISES PROMISES PROMISES

Fig 23 ▲ Shaky

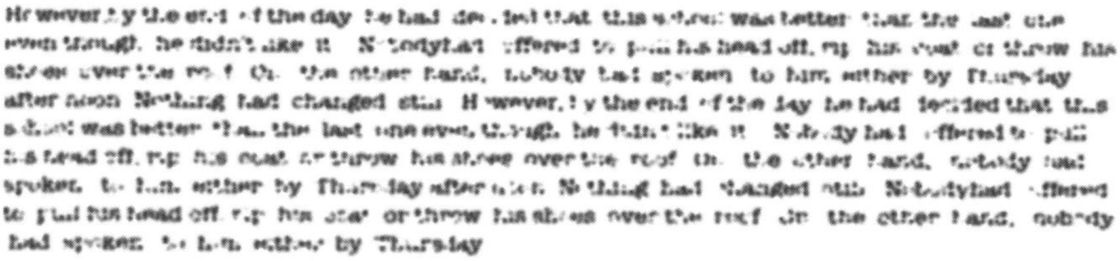

However,by the end of the day he had decided that this school was better than the last one even though, he didn't like it. Nobodyhad offered to pull his head off, rip his coat or throw his shoes over the roof On the other hand, nobody had spoken to him, either by Thursday after noon Nothing had changed still However, by the end of the day he had decided that this school was better than the last one even though, he didn't like it. Nobody had offered to pull his head off, rip his coat or throw his shoes over the roof On the other hand, nobody had spoken to him, either by Thursday after noon Nothing had changed still Nobodyhad offered to pull his head off, rip his coat or throw his shoes over the roof On the other hand, nobody had spoken to him, either by Thursday

Fig 24 ▲ Washout

We all see thingthe same way
We see words in groups or phrases

Fig 25 ▲ Halo

Diagnosis and treatment

✦ The patented Irlen treatment (available only at Irlen Centres by Irlen-trained practitioners, see www.irlenuk.com) uses coloured overlays and precision-tinted filters worn as glasses. The colour can be applied to prescription, non-prescription or safety goggles.

✦ Tinted glasses may also be recommended for reading problems and problems with copying, writing, doing maths, and poor depth perception. The colour of the glasses is usually not the same as the overlay).

✦ The Intuitive Overlays Test has been devised by Professor Wilkins and colleagues at Essex University (among the first to scientifically study the syndrome). It includes a measure of the effect of the coloured overlays on reading speed and accuracy. This method can be carried out by practitioners trained by the Institute of Optometrists.

✦ Coloured overlays are sheets of translucent coloured plastic placed over text. They reduce the contrast and distortions and thus make reading less stressful. Colours range from pale yellow through to bright blue and red, and no one colour suits everyone. Long-term use of overlays is not always necessary, particularly if they are introduced at a young age.

Further information

Irlen, H., *Reading by the Colors*, Penguin Putnam Publishers, New York, 1991.

Wilkins, A., *Reading Through Colour*, John Wiley and Sons Ltd, Chichester, West Sussex, 2003.

The Irlen Institute International HQ, www.irlen.com (accessed 20 September 2005)

www.educational-psychologist.co.uk (click on SEN information) (accessed 20 September 2005)

www.irlenuk.com

➤➤ Language and speech: Development

Language, be it written, gestured or spoken, is a communication skill. It is a code that we learn and then use to communicate ideas, wants and needs to others who also know the code.

Speech is the spoken (oral) form of language.

Components

+ **Oro-motor** functioning: shaping the mouth to produce different sounds; positioning the tongue; the movement of the face muscles; breath control.

+ Phonology: the sounds that make up language (e.g. creating words from sounds).

+ Grammar and syntax: altering meaning by adding to words (e.g. girl + -s = girls; walk + -ed = walked) or changing word order (e.g. I hit the boy/the boy hit me).

+ Semantics: the meanings of words, phrases and sentences.

+ Pragmatics: using language for different situations (e.g. having a conversation, telling a story).

+ Prosody: intonation, stress, rhythm.

Language development guidelines

+ By about 6 months: babbling, tracking sounds, smiling, differentiated crying.

+ By about 9 months: sound combinations (e.g. ma-ma); gestures (e.g. pointing, reaching); reacts to tones of voice; copies sounds.

+ By about 1 year: vocalises to self; 1-word utterances emerge; generalised use of 1 word (e.g. joos = water, milk, drink, thirsty); points and vocalises to obtain objects; follows simple instruction paired with a gesture (e.g. 'Come to mummy').

+ By about 18 months: 2-word (telegraphic) utterances emerge (e.g. 'Shoes off'); understands and responds to simple questions or instructions (e.g. 'Where's your shoe?'); speech not always intelligible.

+ By 3 years: recognisable sentence structure, grammar and pragmatic language emerging (using more words for more precise meaning e.g. 'I my drink now!'); can follow two requests ('Get the ball and put it on the table'); speech increasingly clear, but with common sound substitutions (e.g. yeth/yes, wiv/with).

+ 3–4 years: speech clearer; vocabulary expanding; misapplies/generalises rules (e.g. uses the '-ed' ending indiscriminately – 'I losted my ball'); use of 'why?', not so much to know as to experiment with the power of words to open up a dialogue.

✦ By 5 years: speech easily understood; sentence structure established; an expressive vocabulary of about 2000 words, but understands about 6000; wants to know more; listens to answers to 'why' questions.

✦ By 6 years: coherent, mostly grammatically correct speech; increasing use of language to initiate social interaction and satisfy intellectual curiosity; sound substitutions have usually disappeared.

✦ 6–8 years: language increasingly consists of conventional patterns of speech, gesture, intonation, rhythm; child is increasingly able to understand the 'subtleties' of language (e.g. they can tell and appreciate simple jokes and plays on words).

Further information

The Speech, Language and Hearing Centre, www.speech-lang.org.uk (accessed 20 September 2005)

➤➤ Language and speech: Difficulties and disorders

Some children do not develop language as expected. When it is not related to any other problem (e.g. *CLEFT PALATE, AUTISM*) it is often referred to as a specific language difficulty. This can coexist with another disability (e.g. a child with a stutter who suffers from an *ATTENTION DEFICIT DISORDER*).

It is estimated that 6 in every 100 children will at some time have a language and/or speech difficulty.

Speech difficulties and **disorder**s affect how well others understand the child and how confident s/he is about speaking. The disorder may fall into one or a combination of the following categories:

✦ articulation/phonological: sound substitutions (e.g. sand/tand), difficulties with sounds in sequence (e.g. bridge/bidge)

✦ dysfluency (*STUTTERING/STAMMERING*): repetitions, hesitations or prolongation of sounds (at the beginning of words, within words) or of entire words or phrases

✦ voice: pitch, volume, quality (e.g. too high, too loud).

Language disorders are problems understanding and/or using words. This may be:

✦ receptive: understanding and/or speed of processing incoming information (e.g. word meanings, instructions)

✦ expressive: putting words together (e.g. omits words, substitutes words, poor vocabulary, poor word retrieval)

✦ mixed expressive/receptive: both understanding and using language effectively

✦ semantic: understanding abstract words and ideas (e.g. feelings), taking words literally (e.g. 'Cut that out!') and picking up on key information (e.g. following directions)

✦ pragamatic: using language socially (e.g. interrupting, talking too much/too little)

✦ semantic-pragmatic: combination of the two areas

✦ word retrieval: recalling and using words, despite knowing their meaning; excessive use of fillers (e.g. um, er); using non-specific words (e.g. 'thingy'); logical word substitutions (e.g. light switch for light bulb); slow when naming things, retelling a story.

Causes

✦ *HEARING* loss: particularly if there is a history of **ear infections**, *ALLERGIES*, colds or other upper respiratory infections.

✦ **Neurological** disorder: can affect **oro-motor** functioning as well as language processing and speech production.

✦ Brain injury: can damage language centres of the brain.

✦ **Intellectual impairment**: can affect the efficiency of overall functioning of the brain.

✦ Physical **impairment**: can affect oro-motor coordination, speech clarity, voice quality, breathing.

✦ Social/environmental factors: sometimes children are not exposed to enough language to learn the rules (e.g. neglected, institutionalised children); sometimes adults respond too quickly to gestures, and the child sees no need to develop other communication skills; sometimes moving from one culture to another can arrest or confuse the development or use of the first language.

Symptoms

Symptoms can include the following:
✦ angry, frustrated, poor attention
✦ jumbled speech, poor clarity
✦ lots of hesitations, 'fillers' (e.g. um, er)
✦ poor eye contact; lack of intonation, expression in voice
✦ skills fall well below developmental expectations; poor learning progress
✦ slow to respond when spoken to
✦ struggle behaviour when speaking (e.g. face, neck muscles move excessively).

Treatment

A *SPEECH AND LANGUAGE THERAPIST* should evaluate the child's language development, design a plan of language learning and carry it out. The Speech and Language Therapist may recommend further evaluation by other professionals (e.g. neuropsychologist, paediatrician, ear, nose and throat specialist, *EDUCATIONAL PSYCHOLOGIST*).

Further information

I CAN, www.ican.org.uk (accessed 20 September 2005)

►► Laterality

Laterality is a part of body image (how we see ourselves, how we organise ourselves in space). Specifically it is the development of a preference for right-side or left-side eye, ear, hand and leg action (known as lateral dominance).

Brain function

The left hemisphere (half) of the brain is generally responsible for speech and language, verbal memory, decision-making, hearing and right-side body messages. The right side controls tactile sensations, visual-spatial information, emotion and left-side messages. The Corpus Callosum integrates the hemispheres (see figure 26).

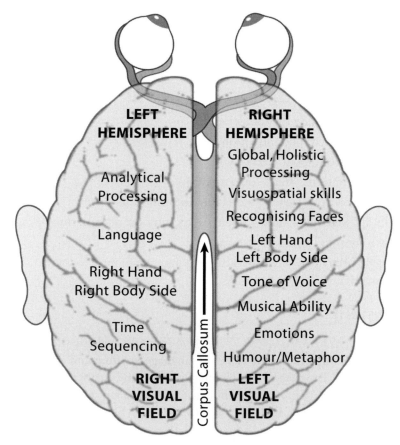

Fig 26 ▲ The hemispheres of the human brain

Dominance

Most people have one-sided dominance – their preferred eye, ear, hand and leg are on the same side of the body – and about 20 per cent of people have mixed dominance (e.g. using the right hand and left ear). This does not imply a particular difficulty. Moreover, use of the non-dominant hand for some actions is quite common. For instance, right-handed mothers often hold their babies with their left arm to free the dominant hand to do a more demanding manipulative task (e.g. open a collapsible pushchair).

Cross-laterality/mixed dominance

However, some problems are linked to cross-laterality, particularly in children who are delayed in establishing dominant eye, ear, hand or leg. For example:

✦ difficulty perceiving left and right sides of objects and letters

✦ extreme rotation of writing or reading page

✦ tendency to be disorganised

✦ uncertainty about own left and right body sides

✦ unusual tilt of the head when writing (30–40°).

Crossing the midline

The midline is an imaginary line that divides the left and right sides of the body. Children need to be able to work on the left side of their bodies with their right side (arm, hand, leg, etc.) and vice versa. For example, to write in English (which has a left-to-right convention), both left- and right-handers have to reach across their midline at some point in a smooth, fluent movement.

Young children (under the age of about 5) are not usually able to cross the midline and will therefore swap hands rather than reach across their body, even if they have established *HAND PREFERENCE*. For example, a child who is showing left-hand preference will, until able to reach across the midline, still swap from left to right hand to continue the activity on the right side of the body.

Developmental stages

✦ By 2 years: children can name and touch their tummy, legs, feet, arms, face parts.

✦ By 3 years: children show established hand preference but no awareness of this.

✦ By 4 years: children can name other body parts (e.g. shoulders, elbows).

✦ By 5 years: children are aware of left and right, but cannot tell which is which; they can cross the midline.

✦ By 8 years: children can locate left and right sides on themselves and on others; they demonstrate dominant leg, eye and ear preference.

131

►► Learning aids

There is an ever-increasing list of strategies, methods and ways to make learning easier, more accessible, less stressful and even just more fun. In some instances such learning aids are essential, and while some are expensive, others are not. They may be divided into electronics and specific disability aids and strategies.

Electronics

✦ Options to increase computer screen print size and modify typeface, text colour and background and add coloured overlays, with user profiles stored so that individual children's needs and preferences can be called up each time they use the computer.

✦ Text-to-speech applications that make the computer talk. This helps children hear themselves and others read, as well as helping them to concentrate when reading longer text passages, and reinforcing skills (**multi-sensory** input e.g. spelling rules can be seen and heard simultaneously).

✦ Phonological awareness programmes that encourage auditory information-processing skills. Some have a British English accent, others have an American English accent.

✦ Graded skills packages that teach, encourage or extend literacy and numeracy skills and schemes.

✦ Interactive learning packages that are either complete schemes in themselves or supplementary to traditional reading schemes. Packages often come with talking books (on CD) paired with printed book versions, and interactive material that helps children follow the story visually, aurally and motorically.

✦ Interactive keyboard training programmes that teach young children good keyboard skills, essential for children with physical **impairments** that make handwriting difficult or impossible.

✦ E-books (electronic books) that can be read on standard computers, on personal digital assistants (PDA) or on special e-book readers.

✦ PDAs are portable computers about the size of a telephone that can be used as a word processor, note-taker, calendar, time converter, calculator and personal organiser.

✦ Word processors that are mini laptop size and come with a full keyboard and a screen about the size of a large rear-view mirror. They run basic word-processing programmes, spellchecks, word prediction programmes (that offer vocabulary suggestions) and store word lists (also known as word banks) that the user can create.

- Audio cassette recorders that record onto memory chips rather than tapes, record for several hours and enable recorded material to be transferred into a computer at a higher speed than normal.

- Literacy word banks that are slightly larger than hand-size portable dictionaries, spellcheckers and thesauruses. They often contain common topic words and commonly occurring (high-frequency) words.

- Study skills programmes for older children specifically teach the skills that students with learning difficulties often do not learn easily, if at all, through general teaching (e.g. note-taking, memorising, test revision, essay planning, time management, presentation skills). These programmes are also available in book form.

Specific disability aids and strategies

- Makaton is a communication system for people with a hearing and/or speech and language impairment. It pairs the most frequently needed words for everyday conversation with drawn symbols and with manual signs from British Sign Language. Makaton users are first encouraged to communicate using the symbols and signs to support spoken communication; then gradually the signs and symbols are phased out and speech takes over. Makaton symbols support the written word in the same way that signs support speech. Most of the symbols are black and white and have been designed to show the essential meaning of the words. Makaton is an internationally recognised communication programme.

Fig 27 ▲ Makaton symbol: to read

Fig 28 ▲ Makaton symbol: to write

- Sign language is the cultural language of the deaf community and has its own grammar and syntax. Children who are born deaf or who become deaf before they really develop language will use sign language as their dominant language. Facial expressions, associated gestures and body language are all part of a sign language system. There are sign languages for different countries (e.g. British Sign Language, American Sign Language), although the underlying structure is consistent.

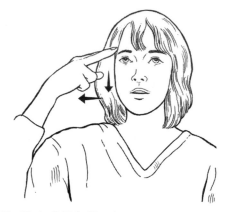

Fig 29 ▲ British Sign Language: name

Fig 30 ▲ British Sign Language: please

✦ Total communication is an approach in deaf education in which any one of a number of communication methods can be used, either singly or in combination, between the deaf child and teachers, parents and friends. Audiological equipment is also used to maximise any hearing the child may have.

✦ Cochlear implants are replacements for the inner ear, intended for people who get little or no benefit from a conventional hearing aid. It consists of a small external microphone that picks up sound and sends it directly to the hearing nerve via a surgically implanted electrode, bypassing the damaged part/s of the ear. In the USA it is an approved medical procedure for children over 2 years.

✦ Cued speech was developed in 1966 because of concerns for the significant literacy problems among deaf children at that time. It was felt that this was the result of poor access to English at a phonemic (phonetic sound) level, essential for reading the English language. The system is made up of hand shapes and hand movements that visually and motorically reinforce where and how consonant and vowel sounds are made. For example, the 't' sound is reinforced by tapping the forefinger against the closed teeth while saying 't'.

✦ Physical impairment aids include sloping writing surfaces, door-opening attachments, adjustable chairs and tables, magnifying rulers, pages with raised lines for extra guidance, pen grips and special pens and pencils.

Further information

Benefits Now, www.benefitsnowshop.co.uk (accessed 20 September 2005)

British Sign Language, www.britishsign.co.uk (accessed 20 September 2005)

Catalogue, www.dyslexic.com (accessed 20 September 2005)

Makaton, www.makaton.com (accessed 20 September 2005)

Royal National Institute for the Deaf, www.rnid.org.uk (accessed 20 September 2005)

Cued Speech Information and Resources, www.cuedspeech.info (accessed 20 September 2005)

➤➤ Middle ear infections

Bacteria and viruses can enter the middle ear via the Eustachian tube (see figure 15) and cause *INFECTIONS*, often when the child has a pre-existing infection (e.g. a cold). Fluid (pus) builds up and presses on the eardrum. This pressure can be painful, and because the eardrum cannot vibrate, there may also be temporary *HEARING* loss. If ear fluid remains after the actual infection has cleared, hearing loss may persist, and research shows that it can affect speech and learning.

Middle ear infections, also known as **otitis media** (OM), are most common in children between 6 months and 2 years. Risk factors include:
+ second-hand tobacco smoke
+ taking a bottle to bed
+ large group settings (e.g. day-care, school), where infections are more difficult to control (OM itself is not contagious)
+ certain conditions (e.g. *CLEFT PALATE, DOWN'S SYNDROME, ALLERGIES*)
+ gender – boys are more prone to OM than girls.

Types

+ Acute (AOM): this starts up quite quickly (rapid onset) and clears fairly swiftly with treatment.
+ Chronic: infection lasts more than 2 weeks; eardrum damage is possible.
+ OME (with effusion): fluid persists for 6 weeks or more after the initial acute OM. The Eustachian tube does not work properly (ventilate) to clear the ear and fluid develops.

Symptoms

These may include:
+ pulling, rubbing ears due to discomfort/pain
+ *FEVER*
+ fussiness, irritability
+ fluid leaking from ear
+ appetite loss
+ sleep disturbances
+ difficulty hearing.

Treatment

Medication can include *ANTIBIOTICS* for bacterial infections and sometimes immunisation against viruses and bacteria that cause recurrent ear infections. Nasal drops and decongestants may help, and antipyretics (to lower temperature) and analgesics (painkillers) may be prescribed.

Ear tube surgery (myringotomy) may be advised for repeated ear infections that do not get better easily and/or there is evidence of hearing loss or speech delay. Small tubes, known as tympanostomy tubes, PE (pressure equalising) tubes or grommets, are put in the eardrum to ventilate (open up) the middle ear blocked by fluid. As the eardrum heals, the tubes are usually pushed out within 6–18 months (depending on the type of tube inserted).

Prognosis

Antibiotics usually work quickly and effectively to clear up AOM.

Ear tubes are successful in treating chronic OM and OME, although research indicates that some children under 2 years who are fitted with ear tubes may need them again.

Further information

Medinfo, www.medinfo.co.uk/conditions (accessed 20 September 2005)

▶▶ Montessori education

The Montessori method is based on the principle that children learn for themselves by exploring what is in their environment. An environment of carefully chosen materials will encourage interaction, work, concentration and enjoyment. Adults must not impose their own special interests on children, making sure that children are introduced to all subjects, materials and experiences so as to develop their own interests.

Background

Maria Montessori was born in Italy in 1870. She was Italy's first female medical doctor; she studied psychology and philosophy and finally became a professor of anthropology. Through her medical practice, her studies and her work with children in Rome, she developed the Montessori Method.

Key points

✦ The learning environment must be carefully thought out and prepared by the teacher.

✦ A crowded, disordered environment causes stress and drains energy.

✦ The teacher puts children in touch with the environment, helping them to research it and make choices.

✦ The environment is arranged according to subject areas (e.g. cooking, library corner).

✦ Children are free to move around, with no time limit for working on a chosen activity.

✦ At any one time in the day, all 'subjects' – maths, language, science, etc. – will be being studied at various levels by all children of mixed ages, learning from each other and from their environment.

✦ The teacher protects the children from interruption.

✦ The teacher observes, facilitates and records children's activities and discoveries, using this information to maintain an appropriate environment.

✦ Materials (games, toys, etc.) must be carefully chosen.

Montessori developmental principles

✦ Birth–6 years: children learn from sensori-motor contact with the environment; toys and materials should be **multi-sensory** and of good quality to encourage children's self-respect, respect for the environment and their appreciation of beauty.

✦ 6–12 years: children are highly productive (e.g. model-making, plays) and the environment must be kept to the essentials to avoid confusion or distraction; sensori-manipulative materials are removed when children are ready to work in the **abstract**.

✦ 12 years +: education becomes more traditional (textbooks, computers, trade tools, etc.) and the environment should now include not only the school but the wider community (e.g. the town, the farm, the public library, the workplace).

Montessori principles are often found in childcare centres, pre-schools, schools and home-schooling programmes, even if the settings are not fully-fledged Montessori centres. Training in Montessori methods is available in many countries.

Further information

www.montessori.edu (accessed 20 September 2005)

Association Montessori Internationale, www.montessori-ami.org (accessed 20 September 2005)

➤➤ Naturopathy

This involves health treatments other than pharmaceutical and surgical interventions. The information below is a sample of the extensive range of naturopathic approaches.

Homeopathy

Homeopathy is a naturopathic system of medicine using dilutions of natural substances to stimulate the body's natural healing processes. In the late eighteenth century it was found that a substance which caused certain symptoms in a healthy individual could cure those symptoms in a sick person; and that by diluting the substance in water, remedies were more powerful.

Classical homeopathy treats the 'whole' person, looking at the mental and emotional aspects of an illness, not just current physical symptoms. Some homeopaths administer combined remedies, the idea being that one of the remedies in the combination will work.

Isopathy is a more recent homeopathy approach. Contemporary drugs and pollutants are diluted and administered to treat either the same disease or the symptoms the drug was designed for.

Osteopathy

Osteopathy is based on the principle that problems in the framework (skeleton) of the body can disturb the body's circulatory and/or nervous system, and so affect health. Osteopaths aim to restore a state of balance and harmony, thus helping the whole person.

Cranial osteopathy is a form of osteopathic treatment that encourages the release of tensions throughout the body, including the head.

Cranio-sacral therapy was developed in 1970 as a gentle method of enhancing the body's own healing capabilities. Through gentle manipulation of the cranial (skull) bones, sacrum (lower back), spinal cord and interconnected membranes and body tissue, cranio-sacral therapy aims to help a wide range of illnesses, pain and dysfunction, while improving circulation and increasing energy.

Anthroposophical Medicine

Based on the work of Rudolf Steiner, this combines artistic, spiritual and scientific insights. It holds that each of us is unique and should be treated accordingly, that loss of meaning or purpose in life leads to ill-health, and that illness can provide positive opportunities for positive life changes.

Further information

www.naturopathy.org.uk (accessed 20 September 2005)

▶▶ Occupational Therapists

An Occupational Therapist (OT) is trained to work with people who, for various reasons, are having difficulties carrying out everyday activities. Occupational Therapists who specialise in working with children commonly evaluate and work with children referred because of:

✦ poor gross- and/or fine-motor skills (balance, *HANDWRITING*, catching/throwing)

✦ problems with attention, concentration, organisation and task completion

✦ difficult social behaviours (overt aggression, high activity levels, over-excitable)

✦ self-help/independent living skills (e.g. dressing/undressing, using a spoon, knife or fork).

The OT can work individually with a child, planning and carrying out a programme that focuses on the specific skills identified in the OT evaluation.

The OT can also work as a consultant, educating parents and others about the reasons for the child's difficulties and how the environment might be adapted to support the child and strengthen problem skills. They demonstrate how to work with the child on specific skills and how to help the child apply skills learned in individual therapy sessions to the mainstream setting.

Evaluation

Typically the OT will gather information from parents and from significant others working with the child and will carry out a variety of activities in individual sessions with the child. Evaluation tools often include parent/carer checklists and **standardised** tests of gross- and fine-motor development and skills (including coordination, posture, muscle tone and strength), sensory profiles (responses to textures, tastes, noises, and so on) and tests of visual and auditory perception.

The OT is able to provide a variety of suggestions and activities that can be used for a group of children, not just the child in therapy; for example, warm-up and relaxation exercises, tactile/sensory walls, work/play stations in the room (e.g. 'snack' area, 'exercise' station, 'hands' work-table). The OT can provide lists of appropriate toys, games and activities for the home as well.

Further information

British Association of Occupational Therapists/College of Occupational Therapists, www.cot.co.uk (accessed 20 September 2005)

➤➤ Pervasive Developmental Disorders (PDD)

PDD is an umbrella term for a number of disorders grouped together because of their diagnostic similarities, as well as the effect they have on the child with the **disorder**.

Disorders

✦ *ASPERGER'S DISORDER*: children with poor communication skills, particularly socially, but with language and *COGNITIVE DEVELOPMENT* which are usually within the **norm**. Verbal language can also be affected (e.g. a little stilted or formal). Children with Asperger's Disorder can have associated learning difficulties, but this is not always the case.

✦ *AUTISM*: children with significant developmental difficulties in language skills (verbal and non-verbal), social interaction skills and unusual, stereotypical behaviours. There is a significant incidence of **intellectual impairment** as well as academic learning difficulties. Autism can vary in severity and impact and it is now often referred to as Autism Spectrum Disorder (ASD).

✦ NOS (not otherwise specified): children with poor non-verbal communication and social interaction and delayed language who may have delayed or impaired development in other areas (e.g. cognitive, motor), but who do not meet the specific criteria for any other PDD.

There are two other PDD conditions that are rarely encountered in mainstream care and education – Rett's **Syndrome** and Childhood Integrative disorder, which have medical criteria in addition to social, language and communication difficulties.

Causes

A PDD is a neurobiological disorder. It may be that there are several different causes resulting in similar sets of characteristics. Pervasive Developmental Disorders are about 4 times more common in boys than in girls.

A PDD is not caused by social or family events (e.g. natural disasters, war, a new sibling, mother returning to work, illness, *DEATH AND GRIEVING* or *DIVORCE AND SEPARATION*).

Characteristics

Despite there being several diagnostic types of PDD, what PDD children have in common is significant difficulty communicating and engaging in social interaction.

✦ Some children do not develop 'normally' from the start; some begin to develop normally, then around 1½ or 2 years seem to withdraw and lose any words they had.

✦ Most children are healthy, with no identifying physical differences that indicate the presence of a disorder (as in *DOWN'S SYNDROME*, for example).

✦ Many children have unusual and inconsistent responses to sound (e.g. very sensitive to some sounds, covering their ears in distress, while seeming to be able to tune out other sounds). Often parents are concerned that their child may be deaf, but testing usually indicates normal hearing.

✦ Some children have specific syndromes or disorders, and a PDD is an additional diagnosis (e.g. *DYSPRAXIA*, **intellectual impairment**, *EPILEPSY*).

✦ Some children have mild motor problems (e.g. a little clumsiness), while others are quite agile.

Diagnosis

Multi-disciplinary assessment by a developmental paediatrician, a *SPEECH AND LANGUAGE THERAPIST*, an audiologist and a psychologist and/or psychiatrist should include:

✦ observing and interacting with the child
✦ collecting developmental, family and health history
✦ a thorough paediatric check-up, including vision and hearing tests
✦ collecting information on behaviour at home and the child's responses to different situations
✦ checklists (e.g. DSM-IV criteria, Childhood Autism Rating Scale, Gillam Asperger's Disorder Scale).

PDD and intellectual impairment

✦ All children with Asperger's Disorder, by definition, have at least normal **intelligence**.

✦ Most children with a PDD have 'uneven' profiles; that is, they are very good in some areas (e.g. puzzles, mechanical tasks, letters, numbers, memory), but have difficulty in other areas (especially communication, **abstract** reasoning).

+ It is thought that about 75 per cent of children with Autism are intellectually impaired (mildly to severely).
+ Children with PDD-NOS may or may not have intellectual impairment.
+ It is often difficult to evaluate the intelligence of very young children with a PDD, due to social, communication and behavioural difficulties.

PDD and family history

Statistically there is a higher chance that siblings of a child with a PDD will also have a PDD.

Prognosis

It is difficult to predict outcome, but research shows that outcome is best for children who:
+ get intensive early schooling
+ have good intelligence
+ develop speech before the age of 5.

Treatment

In general, specialised programmes have the following ingredients:
+ a structured, predictable schedule so the child can anticipate changes in the day
+ relatively few children per teacher
+ emphasis on social communication and language development
+ use of *PLAY* and other group activities to promote social and communication development
+ use of *BEHAVIOUR MANAGEMENT* techniques to help with behavioural problems.

Some forms of PDD (e.g. Asperger's Disorder) do not particularly restrict participation in mainstream settings (e.g. nursery programmes, classrooms), while others may be more problematic and less positive for the child (e.g. moderate or severe Autism). Special needs/mainstream combinations are sometimes possible, whereby the child participates in the regular group at certain times, with individualised intervention at others. Learning specialists can help plan educational programmes.

Parents, carers and teachers often need to develop behaviour management skills with help from behaviour specialists (e.g. **Applied Behaviour Analysis (ABA)** specialists). In addition, *OCCUPATIONAL THERAPISTS* and

SPEECH AND LANGUAGE THERAPISTS can help maximise communication skills and reduce frustration levels.

Other treatment

There is no specific drug to treat PDD, but some medications can treat associated difficulties (e.g. hyperactivity, **anxiety**, self-injurious behaviour), and there are various other potentially helpful therapies available (e.g. art or music *PSYCHOTHERAPY*).

Further information

Yale Child Study Center (Developmental Disabilities Clinic), www.med.yale.edu (click on 'Directories', 'A' in the alphabetical listing, 'Autism/PDD Clinic' and, finally, 'PDD Information' from the column on the left) (accessed 20 September 2006)

➤➤ Physiotherapists

Physiotherapists are trained to work with people who, for various reasons, are having difficulties with mobility (e.g. injuries from accidents, breathing problems including *ASTHMA, CEREBRAL PALSY*). Physiotherapists who specialise in working with children commonly evaluate and work with children referred because of difficulties with:

+ poor gross- and/or fine-motor skills (balance, *HANDWRITING*, catching/throwing)
+ physical **impairment** (e.g. Cerebral Palsy)
+ physical abnormalities (e.g. talipes – club feet)
+ injury (accident, muscle strain).

The Physiotherapist can work individually with a child, planning and carrying out a programme that focuses on the specific skills identified in the physiotherapy evaluation. Therapy can consist of guided exercises, manipulation (movement of joints), water exercise, ultrasound and **acupuncture**. The Physiotherapist can also work as a consultant, educating parents and others about the reasons for the child's difficulties and how the environment might be adapted to support the child and strengthen skills. They demonstrate how to work with the child and how to help the child apply skills learned in individual therapy sessions to the mainstream setting.

Evaluation

Typically, the Physiotherapist will gather information from parents and from significant others working with the child and will carry out a variety of activities in individual sessions with the child, assessing specific physical functions and abilities. Evaluation tools often include parent/carer checklists and **standardised** tests of gross- and fine-motor development and skills (including coordination, posture, muscle tone and strength). The initial assessment is followed by a discussion about immediate and long-term requirements and a plan for appropriate treatment.

Treatment is frequently given in the child's home, using various techniques, such as massage, exercises, neuro-developmental therapy, mobilisation, stretching, strengthening and posture education. The Physiotherapist is able to provide a variety of suggestions and activities that can be used for a group of children, not just the child in therapy (e.g. warm-up and relaxation exercises), and can provide lists of toys, games, activities and appropriate aids (e.g. shoes, furniture) for the home as well.

Further information

The Chartered Society of Physiotherapy, www.csp.org.uk (accessed 20 September 2005)

Therapy World, www.therapy-world.co.uk (accessed 20 September 2005)

➤➤ Piaget, Jean

During the mid-1900s, Jean Piaget developed a theory of *COGNITIVE DEVELOPMENT* (how children learn intellectually), a theory that still shapes many child-care and education settings and activities, adult–child interaction styles and assessments of children's intellectual progress today.

Piaget's theory states that:

✦ children are born with a basic ability to develop cognitions (understandings, concepts, etc.)

✦ they build up schemas (organised ideas/plans) about what they experience

✦ children's cognitions are different to those of adults

✦ cognitions evolve with time and experience into more sophisticated ones that enable the child to deal with the real world

✦ all children pass through **developmental stages** defined by certain behaviours and abilities

✦ what happens in one stage influences what happens in the next

✦ there are certain cognitive processes that children have to go through in order to keep learning.

Cognitive processes

Schemas

There are three main types:

✦ action: reflexes (sucking, grasping, etc.) provide physical interaction and experience

✦ symbolic: words, objects, actions can mean different things/represent something else (e.g. a shoebox is a car)

✦ operational: acting on objects/situations to influence, change, reverse or create outcomes.

Organisation, adaptation, equilibration and disequilibration

✦ Organisation: applying what is known about one situation to another, similar one, thus expanding what is known (e.g. the infant's action to grasp his/her foot can be organised to grasp a toy).

✦ Adaptation: children first assimilate information (take it in and fit it to what they know), then may have to accommodate (adjust what they know in the light of the new information).

✦ Equilibration: a balance between what children know and what they need to know, to deal with/understand new information, problems, and so on.

✦ Disequilibration: when new information 'upsets' this balance in such a way that the child is motivated to begin the organisational, adaptation process again. There is a 'ripple in the pool' effect, with a child's knowledge and understanding spreading ever outwards to eventually encompass the adult world.

Stages

Sensori-motor (birth to 2 years)

✦ Direct sensory experiences (seeing, touching, tasting, etc.).
✦ Exploration of the nearby environment (e.g. reaching for something).
✦ Exploration through repetitive action ('When I did x, y happened – will it happen again?').
✦ Gradual realisation that people and things continue to exist even when they are out of sight (object and person permanency).

Pre-operational (2–7 years)

✦ Emerging ability to mentally imagine people, things and actions.
✦ Increasingly able to order and act on the world (e.g. name, describe and manipulate things, make one thing stand for another).
✦ Learning takes place through action, language (e.g. questioning, talking), *PLAY* (toys, pretend play, cooperative play, formal games, etc.), watching others and imitating them.
✦ Understanding is often confused because of **egocentricity** (unable to see a problem from someone else's point of view) and lack of experience.
✦ Learning is through concrete materials.

Concrete operations (7–11 years)

✦ Children still need hands-on (concrete) experiences to prove what they know, but gradually develop mental reasoning and problem-solving.
✦ Intuitive thought (logical 'guessing') emerges, enabling conservation, reversibility.
  – Conservation enables children to realise that sometimes things remain the same, even if they look different (e.g. 1 large ball of Play-Doh remains the same quantity even if it is divided into 4 smaller balls). We no longer have to see it to believe it.
  – Reversibility is understanding that actions (operations) can go both ways (e.g. 'adding' is the reverse of 'taking away').
  – These two skills allow the child to understand ideas with several attributes (e.g. a cube has length, depth and height).

Formal operations (11 years +)

✦ Children are able to carry out operations mentally, very often without concrete materials (e.g. mental arithmetic: 'A car travels at 60 km/hour. How long will it take to travel 540 km?').

✦ They can reason hypothetically (e.g. 'What would you do if…? /What happens when…?).

✦ They have ideas on **abstract** issues (e.g. justice, morality, conscience).

Piaget today

Piaget's theory gave rise to extensive ideas, experiments and research about cognitive development, and findings now indicate that:

✦ Children can think in more complex ways, at an earlier age, than Piaget believed.

✦ Piagetian theory does not really take cultural differences into account.

✦ Some people, even as adults, never get to be very good at Formal thinking.

✦ There is an overemphasis on the environment as the influencing factor, rather than social factors (e.g. other people's behaviour, modelling, imitation).

Piaget and the child's environment

✦ Young children need a safe, secure environment, because they certainly will want to explore it.

✦ Children need age-appropriate materials if they are to be able to manipulate them and be challenged appropriately by them. It is organised challenge that, according to Piaget, moves them from equilibration to disequilibration and keeps them engaged in learning.

✦ There need to be opportunities for exploration and experimentation, again pitched at the right level, so that these activities are both pleasurable and rewarding.

✦ There need to be a number of different ways to be successful at a task.

✦ The environment needs to be changed according to the child's developing skills, knowledge and interests.

✦ Adults need to know where a child is 'at' developmentally if they are to make good choices about environment, materials, activities, and so on.

Further information

Piaget's developmental theory, www.learningandteaching.info/learning/piaget.htm (accessed 20 September 2005)

➤➤ Play

It is generally agreed that play implies a sense of enjoyment (which can come from relaxing, time alone, relief from anxiety, doing nothing, problem-solving, interacting with others, humour, and so on); also that it contributes to development, that there are identifiable stages of play and that the play behaviours and activities of children can reveal where they are 'at' developmentally (motorically, cognitively, emotionally, and so on).

There are four main stages of play:

✦ Practice/sensori-motor, exploration play: birth to 2 years

Touching, mouthing, moving, seeing, listening, and so on, all expand awareness and enjoyment of the environment.

✦ Symbolic/pre-operational, pretend play: 2–7 years

Objects are investigated, grouped, manipulated and used to represent something else (e.g. a shoebox is a car); children imagine themselves as someone else (e.g. cartoon characters); children begin to explore real life (e.g. playing house), act out worrying situations (e.g. adult arguments), explore what they can create (construction toys) and gain sensory pleasure and develop a sense of body image (finger plays, action songs).

✦ Games with rules/concrete: 7–11 years

Children are less **egocentric** (e.g. take turns, share), understand about winning, use play to turn formal learning into fun (e.g. board games), enjoy team games, and like putting on 'concerts'.

✦ Adolescent play: the teenage years

Team games, excelling (sports, music), choosing own leisure activities, language (innuendo, joke telling), imitating real-life 'heroes' (e.g. pop stars) through dress and mannerisms.

Play behaviours

These can occur in isolation or in combination, across stages:

✦ unoccupied: idling, no obvious purpose (e.g. rolling on floor)
✦ purposeful: activity has an obvious purpose (e.g. construction toys)
✦ solitary: playing alone quite happily, self-absorbed
✦ onlooker: watching others with genuine interest but not joining in
✦ parallel: playing at own activity alongside each other, occasionally interacting but not sharing
✦ imitating: copying actions, language and mannerisms of others

- ✦ symbolic: using what is at hand to stand for a real object or an imaginary setting (e.g. my cars are going up the hill = 2 empty matchboxes being 'driven' over a pile of books)
- ✦ sharing/associative play: playing at own activity but sharing resources (e.g. blocks)
- ✦ pretend: playing houses, schools (using real and pretend objects to set the scene)
- ✦ social/cooperative/group: actively seeking the company of others (e.g. board games, sports).

Where a child differs radically from age and stage expectations, it may be necessary to teach aspects of play. Play is often the medium of various psychotherapeutic approaches (e.g. play, art and music therapies).

Further information

Children's Hospital of Wisconsin, www.chw.org (search item: play stages) (accessed 20 September 2005)

➤➤ Prematurity

The ideal time from conception to birth is 40 weeks. Infants are considered premature if they are born at less than 37 weeks or if they weigh less than 2.5 kg (even if they are born at full-term). The shorter the time **in utero** and the lower the birth weight, the higher the risk of complications, although prematurity does not always lead to problems.

Critical foetal development

The unborn baby develops on a continuum (a continuous scale over time), but certain aspects of development are more vulnerable at certain times during the pregnancy. For example, in the first 12 weeks, the organs (eyes, ears, heart, and so on) are in a phase of critical growth and, as such, are at greater risk of damage from trauma (e.g. exposure to rubella/measles in the first 2–3 months of the pregnancy).

From 20 weeks onwards many of the organs are formed and damage is then more likely to be to the growth and proportion of body structures (arms, legs) and to the actual functioning of the organs.

Higher-risk factors for premature babies at birth

✦ Very premature (the shorter the time in utero, the greater the risk)
✦ Low birth weight (<1500 g)
✦ Breathing difficulties
✦ Feeding problems (sucking, swallowing, etc.)
✦ *INFECTIONS*
✦ High/low body temperature
✦ Brain damage and/or physical **impairment** (blindness, deafness, *CEREBRAL PALSY*).

Development 0–2 years

The time from birth to approximately 2 years of age is a critical time in all children's lives, but for premature infants it is considered to be particularly so because it is also the 'catch-up' period. Over this 2-year period some delays or difficulties not necessarily evident at birth may be noted in:

✦ body weight and height
✦ physical coordination
✦ dental structure (e.g. teeth, palate)
✦ feeding/eating skills

- ◆ *LANGUAGE AND SPEECH* development
- ◆ *COGNITIVE DEVELOPMENT*
- ◆ *SOCIAL-EMOTIONAL DEVELOPMENT.*

Delays and/or difficulties are not always serious, however, and some children will simply take a little longer to catch up than others.

A child born at 32 weeks (about 7 months), for example, is really about 2 months younger (in development) than his/her full-term peers, and so may well not be at quite the same developmental level in these first 2 years or so.

Moreover, premature children (like all children) inherit things like height and weight, so there has to be a balance between what is a worrying delay and what is not.

Sometimes an early-years programme of stimulation is recommended, especially where there are clear signs of developmental delay (e.g. physiotherapy, speech and language enrichment, *PLAY* activities).

Further information

Premature Baby – Premature Child, www.prematurity.org (accessed 20 September 2005)

▶▶ Psychology

Psychology is the study of the thoughts, feelings and reasons behind the way people act, react and interact. Psychologists are trained in scientific methods: observing, measuring, *TESTING* and using **statistics** to show that what is found is reliable and not just a matter of chance. They are also trained in the facts and various theories of behaviour and how to use them to help people manage the difficulties they are facing.

Psychologists work in health and social care settings (e.g. hospitals, health centres, child and adolescent mental health services and social services). They can work in public organisations, private practice or both. They may work with the child, with the parents and other family members, either as individuals or as groups. They can also act as consultants to childcare and education settings, advising them on how to help children with particular difficulties (e.g. *BEHAVIOUR MANAGEMENT*, management of stress or grief).

Psychologists specialising in working with children are concerned with practical problems, such as helping children deal with their parents' *DIVORCE AND SEPARATION, DEATH AND GRIEVING*, disability, learning difficulties and behaviour problems. They may also refer children to other professionals as needed (e.g. *OCCUPATIONAL THERAPISTS, PHYSIOTHERAPISTS*, learning support).

There are several types of Psychologists who work with children; for example:

✦ Clinical Psychologists work with children referred because of mental or physical health problems (e.g. **anxiety**, depression, behaviour **disorder**s, personal and family relationships).

✦ Counselling Psychologists work with children referred for various reasons, including bereavement, family problems and mental health problems (e.g. anxiety or a **phobia**). Counselling Psychologists explore the underlying issues and aim to develop a relationship with the child that helps them work together.

✦ *EDUCATIONAL PSYCHOLOGISTS* use a wide range of testing techniques to evaluate and help children who have various difficulties in the care and education setting (e.g. learning, social/behavioural difficulties). Services include assessment, further referral, planning learning and behaviour management programmes, as well as supporting the child, the parents and others at home and in the wider care and education community.

◆ Neuro-psychologists apply their psychological training and skills specifically to help brain-damaged and brain-injured people. Neuro-psychologists working with children assess the effect of the injury on the child's social, emotional and educational abilities and functioning, and make recommendations for the types of support services that are most appropriate.

Further information

The British Psychological Society, www.bps.org.uk (accessed 20 September 2005)

➤➤ Psychotherapy

Psychotherapy involves a personal relationship between the client and the therapist, where the client feels safe enough to talk about problems and express often difficult feelings. Psychotherapy can be useful for a wide range of problems, including DEPRESSION, **anxiety** and behaviour problems; there are a variety of psychotherapeutic approaches available.

Art therapy

Art therapy uses artwork and the creative process involved in producing art (e.g. the materials, how they are used) as a means of expression and communication, thus adding another dimension to the verbal relationship between the child and the therapist.

Art therapy is largely non-directed (i.e. no suggestions are made about what to make), and artwork is not usually analysed by the therapist. Rather, the therapist and the child 'learn' its meaning together.

Artwork made in therapy is usually confidential and the child can go back to it at will, to think about it and talk about it. In addition, the artwork often contains difficult experiences, and by keeping the artwork within therapy sessions, these experiences are also contained, and hopefully the child is therefore less fearful about them and can deal with them more successfully.

Cognitive behaviour therapy (CBT)

This is based on the principle that people with depression have confused views of themselves and the world. CBT focuses on changing these cognitive confusions.

Anxiety **disorder**s are another focus of CBT, and both individual and family therapy can be used. Such disorders are associated with a genetic factor (60–80 per cent of children with anxiety disorders come from families with a similar history), and with 'anxiety-enhancing' parent behaviour. Family CBT aims to decrease child anxiety, parental anxiety, and anxiety-enhancing behaviours (e.g. overprotection).

Dance movement therapy

This involves children in a creative process aimed at their emotional, cognitive, physical and social integration. The dance movement therapist encourages the child to explore the emotional experiences that accompany movement and changes to movement.

Dance movement therapy can be used for a variety of problems, including conflict, communication skills (particularly for feelings or experiences difficult to communicate by words alone), concerns about body image (e.g. *EATING DISORDERS*, physical **impairment**) and anxieties about physical contact or trust.

Family therapy

Family therapy holds that individuals and families are 'systems' or units and that a child's problem (e.g. behaviour, depression) is influenced by individuals within a system (e.g. a family, a cultural group). The therapist works not only with the individual but with the relevant external system/s (e.g. the family, the school), because unless they modify their behaviours (which are reinforcing the child's problems), the child will not change.

Interpersonal therapy (IPT)

This focuses on working through disturbed personal relationships that may contribute to *DEPRESSION IN CHILDREN AND ADOLESCENTS*. The therapist helps the child to evaluate his/her interactions and behaviours with others, to understand them and to make decisions about them (e.g. how to do things differently, communicate better).

Music therapy

Music therapy uses music experiences to help with physical, psychological, cognitive, behavioural and/or social functioning. Music therapists work with individual children, small groups, staff and parents. Often, music therapy enables teachers or the family to see a difficult child in a new light and offers them, and the child, new ways of interacting.

Music therapists involve children in singing, listening, moving and playing, and in creative activities, exploring which styles of music, techniques and instruments are most effective or motivating for each child, and building on the child's spontaneous play to address areas of need.

Play therapy

This helps children to explore their feelings, to express themselves and to make sense of their life experiences. Some therapies prove inappropriate for children who struggle to put their feelings into words, whereas play is children's natural medium to learn, communicate and explore. Play therapy is most often used for children aged 3–12 years.

Play therapists generally work with individual children, but can also work with groups and with siblings. Activities can include art, storytelling, sand-play, music, dance and movement, puppets and masks.

Play therapy sessions usually take place once a week, at the same time, at the child's home, care setting, school or clinic. It can be a short- or long-term intervention, according to each child's needs.

Psychoanalysis

While not commonly used with young children, a brief mention of psychoanalysis is included here for the sake of clarification.

Psychoanalysis is a form of psychotherapy, not psychotherapy itself. It is based on the work of Sigmund Freud and takes the view that two factors underlie social and emotional difficulties – past events (developmental trauma and life experiences) and present stresses (both inside the person and outside, e.g. school). Past and present factors are hard to separate, however, because current problems are layered on top of the old, unresolved problems that a person has had for a long time (often without realising it).

The psychoanalyst tries to help the person discuss, analyse and resolve the old issues so that the present problems can also be resolved.

Further information

Art therapy: Art Therapy in School Service, www.atiss.co.uk (accessed 20 September 2005)

Counselling and psychotherapy: British Association for Counselling and Psychotherapy, www.bacp.co.uk (accessed 20 September 2005)

Dance movement therapy: The Association for Dance Movement Therapy UK, www.admt.org.uk (accessed 20 September 2005)

Family therapy: Association for Family Therapy and Systemic Practice in the UK, www.aft.org.uk (accessed 20 September 2005)

Music therapy: British Society for Music Therapy, www.bsmt.org (accessed 20 September 2005)

Play therapy: The United Kingdom Society for Play and Creative Arts Therapies, www.playtherapy.org.uk (accessed 20 September 2005); British Association of Play Therapists, www.bapt.info (accessed 20 September 2005)

Psychoanalysis: Mental Health and Psychology Directory, PsychNet-UK.com (accessed 20 September 2005)

Psychotherapy: Institute of Psychotherapy and Social Studies, www.ipss-psychotherapy.org (accessed 20 September 2005)

►► Refugee and asylum-seeker children

By legal definition, refugees are people who have left their own country for another country for various hardship reasons, and who are protected from being returned to their country of origin. Asylum-seekers have also crossed an international border to another country in search of safety and refugee status, and are waiting for the government of that country to make a decision about them.

This entry will use UK examples and data sources, but should not be seen as relevant only to the UK or other English-speaking countries.

Special needs

Needs may relate to living conditions in their country of origin (e.g. war, famine) and/or to coping with a new country (new language, rules, cultural expectations) and the attitudes and assumptions of those they meet.

+ Some children are traumatised by events and/or are grieving.
+ Some just need the reassurance of somewhere to live, something to eat and the daily routine of school and play, and so on.
+ Some children are unaccompanied or live with extended family members, and are without parents and/or siblings.
+ Some children had interrupted care and education in their country of origin.
+ Parents may not know about health, care and education services for their children in their new country and may not have enough dominant language to find out about them.
+ These children may arrive at odd times in the school year and then may have to move again, perhaps several times, in quick succession.
+ They may have to wait for a place in a local care setting, playgroup, kindergarten, and so on, and by the time a place becomes available they have to move away.
+ Parents themselves are experiencing a range of uncertainties and fears and can communicate this to the children and/or neglect their children.
+ Children may be living in substandard housing, the family may not have employment (illegal in the UK for asylum-seekers) and may not have income for adequate food, clothing, school books, and so on (a 2002 report from the Refugee Council and Oxfam found that 85 per cent of a UK sample refugee population experienced hunger on a regular basis).

Meeting the needs

Early-years provision

In the UK, the age profile of refugee communities is younger than the non-refugee population, and so it is highly probable that there are more children under 5 in these communities than in the population as a whole. Thus childcare and early schooling experiences can play a significant role in meeting particular needs; for example:

✦ provide dominant-language exposure at a young age, reducing the likelihood of later school failure and saving on the cost of future EAL needs

✦ provide free time for parents to attend English language classes, retrain, look for work and have some time out from the stresses of raising young children and living in a foreign community.

Information

Lack of information in the first languages of refugee groups is a significant factor. Therefore, it is important to:

✦ provide translated leaflets and posters (e.g. in the local supermarket, church or mosque, ethnic support group centre)

✦ at parent/teacher meetings, ask if there are younger children at home who might like to go to a nursery group to play with other children

✦ encourage parents to visit care and education settings, especially if they are fearful of differences to their cultural or religious way of life.

Social-emotional well-being

There are various ways of helping children to relax, make friends and learn the dominant language; for example:

✦ *PLAY* groups and play therapy: many refugee children will have had play experiences interrupted or have had no experience of them at all; those living in temporary housing (e.g. hostels) may not have space to play; play may not be valued in the culture of origin, and parents and other family members may need help to understand its benefits

✦ after-school clubs, lunchtime clubs, parent-and-toddler groups, toy libraries

✦ referrals to appropriate professionals if there is concern for a child's physical and/or mental health, learning or behaviour (being mindful, however, of the family reaction and interpretation of such a referral).

Misconceptions, assumptions, discrimination and prejudice

These can exist between the dominant community and the refugee community (in either direction), as well as within ethnic groups, and are often based on religion, cultural practices, language or fear. The following points are important:

✦ explain early-years and school programmes and procedures to parents/family members, and ask about their concerns, with an interpreter present if need be

✦ learn about the practices and expectations of a child's family, culture and religion, and share this with other teachers, parents and the wider community, as appropriate

✦ deal with teasing and *BULLYING* as you would in any other instance

✦ where there are traditional practices that are illegal in the country of residence (e.g. female circumcision is illegal in the UK, but accepted in some other countries), it may be impossible to actually stop it (e.g. it is done in secret); then it is possible only to understand and be sensitive to the implications (e.g. painful menstruation); there are also groups within ethnic communities that can often offer advice.

Further information

Rutter, J., *Working with Refugee Children*, 2003, Joseph Rowntree Foundation, www.jrf.org.uk/bookshop (accessed 2005)

National Association for Language Development in the Curriculum, www.naldic.org.uk (accessed 20 September 2005)

The following 2 sites incorporate information about gypsy and traveller children:

Exchange House Travellers Service, www.exchangehouse.ie/uk.htm (accessed 20 September 2005)

Friends, Families and Travellers, www.gypsy-traveller.org (accessed 20 September 2005)

➤➤ Selective Mutism: An overview

Selective Mutism (SM) is a childhood **anxiety disorder** characterised by the inability to speak in certain social settings, such as school. These children are able to talk normally in settings where they are comfortable, secure and relaxed.

Over 90 per cent of children with SM also have social **phobia**, with an actual fear of social interaction when there is an expectation to talk.

Causes

The majority of SM children have:

+ a family history of anxiety
+ a severely inhibited temperament (at the extreme end of the spectrum for timidity and shyness)
+ a strong probability of very low excitability tolerance, controlled by the area of the brain called the amygdala (faced with a fearful situation, the amygdala sets off protective reactions, and for SM children, fearful situations are social settings).

Selective mutism is *not* caused by the following:

+ *BILINGUALISM*: while some SM children do come from bilingual families, these children are usually very shy and anxious in temperament, and the stress of speaking another language or being in another country increases their anxiety level, resulting in mutism
+ coexisting *LANGUAGE AND SPEECH* disorders or other learning difficulties
+ *CHILD ABUSE*, neglect or trauma (while a child in these circumstances might stop speaking, mutism is not considered a social phobia, but the result or a symptom of trauma).

Symptoms

Symptoms may include:

+ blank facial expression (e.g. lack of smiling, staring into space) when anxious
+ behaviours at home can include moodiness, inflexibility, procrastination, crying easily, bossiness and extreme talkativeness
+ difficulty initiating play with other children
+ difficulty with basic social exchanges (e.g. saying/gesturing thank you, hello, goodbye)

- excessive worry and fears (more often in children over 6 years)
- frozen appearance, awkward and stiff, tense body language (when anxious)
- heightened sensitivity to surroundings/noise/crowds/touch
- history of severe anxiety, frequent tantrums, crying, moodiness, inflexibility, *SLEEP PROBLEMS* and extreme shyness, from infancy onwards
- introspective, sensitive (e.g. acute awareness of other people's feelings, despite difficulty communicating this)
- not speaking
- poor eye contact (when anxious)
- seemingly intelligent, perceptive and inquisitive
- slowness to respond (i.e. when asked a question, will take longer than the average child to respond either non-verbally or verbally, which can make **standardised** *TESTING* difficult and unreliable).

Further information

Selective Mutism Group – Child Anxiety Network, www.selectivemutism.org (accessed 20 September 2005)

▶▶ Selective Mutism: Diagnosis

The average age of diagnosis is between 3 and 8 years. Parents may notice early on that their child does not speak to most people outside the home, and seek advice, or they may think that it is just because the child is very shy. When the child goes to day-care or school, where there is an expectation to interact and speak, carers might tell the parents the child is not interacting with other children. Further advice should be sought if mutism persists for more than a month.

Evaluation

This is carried out by a trained professional and consists of:

◆ parental interview, with emphasis on social interaction, developmental history (including any delays in *HEARING, LANGUAGE AND SPEECH*), behavioural characteristics, family history (especially history of family members with **anxiety**/depression and/or shy temperament), home-life description (family stress, *DIVORCE AND SEPARATION, DEATH AND GRIEVING*, etc.) and medical history

◆ time spent with the child, building up a relationship if possible and observing at first hand

◆ language evaluation (20–30 per cent of selectively mute children have a subtle abnormality with speech and language)

◆ complete physical exam (including hearing).

In addition, **standardised** *TESTING* and psychological assessment may be recommended, especially where the diagnosis is not clear.

Diagnostic criteria

◆ The child does not speak in select places (e.g. school, social events).

◆ The child can speak normally in settings where s/he is comfortable, for example, home (although some SM children can be mute at home).

◆ The inability to speak interferes with functioning in educational and/or social settings.

◆ Mutism has persisted for at least one month.

◆ Mutism is not caused by trauma (e.g. *CHILD ABUSE*), a communication disorder (e.g. *STUTTERING/STAMMERING*) or other disorders (e.g. *AUTISM*).

Prognosis

With early diagnosis and appropriate treatment, the prognosis is very
positive, but if a child remains mute for many years, not talking becomes a
habit, and one that is very hard to break. Moreover, left untreated, SM can
lead to worsening anxiety and a range of social, emotional and behaviour
difficulties (e.g. depression, school refusal).

Treatment strategies

The main goal is to lower anxiety, increase **self-esteem** and increase
confidence in social settings. All expectations for verbalisation should be
removed. Treatment often combines:

+ behavioural strategies
+ short-term medication (to reduce anxiety levels)
+ cognitive behaviour therapy and other forms of *PSYCHOTHERAPY* (e.g.
  art, music)
+ school understanding and involvement
+ family involvement and acceptance of the problem (e.g. sometimes
  parents cannot believe that their child, so chatty at home, is selectively
  mute at school).

►► Sensory Integrative Dysfunction and therapy

Sensory integration is the ability to take in information through the senses, put it together with what we already know and then respond in an organised way. Significant problems organising sensory information may be diagnosed as Sensory Integrative Dysfunction, or Sensory Processing Disorder, a diagnosis and therapy approach based on the work of Dr Jean Ayres.

Characteristics

These may include:

✦ clumsiness/apparent carelessness

✦ delays in academic **achievement**

✦ delays in speech, language or motor skills

✦ difficulty changing from one situation to another

✦ easily distracted

✦ impulsive, poor self-control

✦ over/under-reactive to touch, movement, sight or sound

✦ unable to unwind or calm self

✦ unusually high/low activity levels.

Diagnosis

Evaluation is usually carried out by *OCCUPATIONAL THERAPISTS* or *PHYSIOTHERAPISTS* who have additional training in Sensory Integrative Dysfunction. Keeping **developmental stages** and expectations in mind, evaluation considers the following:

✦ Attention and regulatory skills

   a Can the child screen out irrelevant information (e.g. noises, sights, smells), focus on tasks, accept routines and respond in a balanced way to stimuli?

✦ Sensory defensiveness

   a Tactile intolerance (e.g. combing hair, clothing textures, food temperature).

   b Overreactions to everyday sounds (e.g. putting their hands over their ears).

   c Hypersensitivity to light, poor eye contact.

   d Poor vestibular tolerance balance (e.g. the child is unusually afraid to go down steps).

+ Activity levels

  a Lack of purposeful activity (e.g. dumps blocks out of a box but does not stop to visually examine them or play with them).

  b Little exploratory behaviour (e.g. child sits and watches although physically able to move and interact).

  c Little variety in play, repetitive/stereotypic play (e.g. lines up toy cars but does not move them around, make car noises, etc.).

  d Speed/recklessness (e.g. a history of bumps, stitches, broken bones).

  e Poor protective reflexes (e.g. hands do not go out to break a fall).

  f Inefficient arousal mechanisms (e.g. high activity levels maintained long after the event, extreme difficulty falling asleep, twirls round and round without getting dizzy, jumps excessively).

+ Behaviours

  a Often considered naughty or difficult to handle, not popular with other children.

  b The child often has poor **self-image** and other behavioural problems (e.g. aggression, isolation).

Therapy

Sensory Integrative Therapy, carried out by trained therapists, guides the child through sensory activities that challenge the ability to make successful, organised responses. Physical education, movement education and gymnastics are not the same as Sensory Integrative Therapy.

Further information

The SPD Network, www.spdnetwork.org (accessed 20 September 2005)

Trott, Maryann Colby *et al.*, *SenseAbilities: Understanding Sensory Integration*, Communication Skill Builders, Tucson, AZ, 1993.

➤➤ Sleep: Problems

Children between 1 and 5 years generally need about 10–12 hours' sleep each day, and school-aged children approximately 10 hours (keeping individual differences in mind, of course). When a child does not get enough sleep, it can affect their emotional and physical well-being and this can spill over to daytime activities (e.g. easily upset, falling asleep in class, poor concentration).

Symptoms

Symptoms of sleep problems include:
+ *BED-WETTING*
+ daytime sleepiness
+ difficulty falling asleep
+ frequent waking during the night
+ nightmares and/or night fears
+ talking during sleep
+ teeth grinding and clenching
+ waking early
+ waking up crying.

Common sleep problems

+ Sleep onset association **disorder**: this is related to bedtime expectations (e.g. going to sleep with a night-light). If the child goes to sleep, then wakes after a while and the condition associated with going to sleep is no longer present (e.g. the light has been switched off), s/he wakes fully and becomes distressed.
+ Developmental stage: for example, if separation anxiety is a developmental feature of a child who at the same time is being moved into her/his own room (having been in a cot in the parents' room), then the combination of the two events could cause sleep problems.
+ Nightmares: the child remembers nightmares, which are usually threatening. Girls are affected more often than boys.
+ Night fears: the child is afraid of the night-time and what it might bring (e.g. the dark, parents going out, monsters) and so resists going to bed/sleep.
+ Sleep terrors: the child screams uncontrollably and appears to be awake, but is confused and cannot communicate. Sleep terrors usually begin between the age of 4 and 12 years.

◆ Sleepwalking: children appear to be awake as they move around, but are actually asleep. Sleepwalking usually begins between ages 6 and 12. Sleep terrors and sleepwalking are inherited and boys are more susceptible. In general, children have a single or occasional episode. There is more concern for repeated episodes, and when it affects daytime behaviour.

◆ Social/emotional problems: sleep problems can be related to mood disorders, *ATTENTION DEFICIT DISORDERS* and **anxiety**.

◆ Sleep apnoea: the child stops breathing for a few seconds at a time when sleeping.

◆ Sleep-wake reversal/delayed sleep-phase syndrome: night sleep is almost impossible and day sleep is excessive.

◆ Seasonal Affective Disorder (SAD): lack of sufficient sunlight (e.g. in winter) interferes with normal routines. Treatment with 'bright light' therapy is often successful.

Prognosis

Children usually get over common sleep problems as they mature. However, ongoing concerns should be discussed with a professional (e.g. paediatrician, psychologist).

Further information

Patient UK, www.patient.co.uk/showdoc/560 (accessed 20 September 2005)

➤➤ Sleep problems: Management

In general, persistent sleep problems benefit from professional advice (e.g. a paediatrician, psychologist), who may offer some of the following strategies and suggestions.

Sleep-onset association disorder

+ Natural onset: the child is put to bed when drowsy but still awake, coinciding with *natural* sleep onset rather than a set bedtime hour.
+ Delayed intervention (not considered appropriate management for children under 12 months): the time the carer remains away from a child at sleep-time is gradually increased (several seconds at first, depending on child/carer comfort levels). After each interval away, the child is reassured without being picked up, and without turning on the light. After comforting the child for a minute or two, the carer again leaves the room, even if the child is still crying. Listening to a baby cry for just a minute can feel like forever, so looking at a watch with a second-hand might be suggested.

Night terrors

+ Intervention should be very gentle (e.g. quietly guiding the child back to bed, ideally without waking, since night terrors can be prolonged by trying to wake the child).
+ Safety precautions need to be considered (e.g. windows, doors leading outside).
+ Night terrors can sometimes be confused with **nocturnal seizures**.
+ Frequent or dramatic night terrors may, on rare occasions, warrant medication.

Short sleep requirement

Some children simply do not need as much sleep as others, but this does not always fit in with other routines (e.g. other family members, nursery rest-times). One approach is to change bedtime/rest-time expectations (e.g. the child goes to bed at a set time but can read/play/listen to music for a time; move sleep/wake times around by 30 minutes).

Sleep onset anxiety

A simple but common cause is worry about something that happened that day and a little extra attention at bedtime can help. Deeper **anxiety** can come from frightening news stories/TV programmes or stressful events (e.g. a death in the family). More severe stressors (e.g. *CHILD ABUSE*) may also be at the root of the problem.

Obstructive sleep apnoea

Tiredness caused by obstructive sleep apnoea (where the child stops breathing for a few seconds at a time while sleeping) may lead to increased daytime napping or notable behaviour changes (e.g. increased irritability). Investigate a sleep position that minimises snoring and have the child's *ADENOIDS* and *TONSILS* checked, as well as investigating possible *ALLERGIES.*

➤➤ Social-emotional development

Social development is about learning the behaviours (physical, verbal, moral, etc.) that are expected and accepted by the wider society we live in. Emotional development is about the feelings and ideas that we have about ourselves and other people that make us want to become a part of society. Thus, when children are struggling with social behaviours, it may be that they have misunderstood a 'rule' or that perhaps they have negative feelings about themselves (e.g. poor **self-esteem**) or mistrust others.

Eric Erikson developed an eight-stage theory connecting children's development of social skills to how they feel/think/reason about themselves and about others in their world; that is, their emotional **cognition**. In each stage certain important cognitions develop as a result of experiences. These experiences can be positive or negative, making socialisation more pleasant and successful, or less so; and what happens in one stage affects development in the next stage.

Four of Erikson's stages cover the developmental period from birth to about 11 years.

Birth–2 years (trust versus mistrust)

Trust comes from having needs met (changing a wet nappy, regular meals, warmth, etc.); from people responding to social signals (e.g. lifting arms to be picked up, first words, smiles); from being able to explore in a safe environment. The child who trusts will reach out and want to know more and to interact more.

2–4 years (autonomy versus doubt)

Autonomy (independence) comes from being encouraged to explore the environment; from being helped to establish control over things like toileting (but not being punished for toileting 'accidents'); from experiencing patience and a sense of security in which to explore. The autonomous child will be increasingly confident and at ease in the social environment.

4–6 years (initiative versus guilt)

Initiative comes from praise and attention for developing own ideas and solutions to problems and for being more independent; from social success (e.g. using turn-taking, sharing); from encouragement to try new things; from the feeling that there is still someone there to 'catch' you if things go wrong. The child with initiative will be self-confident and have positive self-esteem in social interactions.

6–11 years (industry versus inferiority)

A sense of industry comes from being more independent; from self-discipline (e.g. doing homework); from learning formal school skills (e.g. reading) and being able to use these skills to follow individual interests; from discovering the pleasure in participating socially for one's own sake, not because adults say so. The industrious child is trusting, independent, likes being busy, is able to accept direction and enjoys being part of a group.

Further information

King's Psychology Network, www.psyking.net/id161.htm (accessed 20 September 2005)

➤➤ Social Workers

Social Workers are trained to work as advisers, advocates, counsellors or listeners, with the aim of enabling people to live successfully within their local communities by helping them find solutions to their problems.

Social Workers specialising in working with children typically evaluate and support children in the following circumstances:

✦ family relationships and difficulties (e.g. keeping families together, helping children with bereavement or illness in the family, unemployment, housing)

✦ *ADOPTION* and fostering

✦ risk to health and safety (e.g. *CHILD ABUSE*)

✦ younger people leaving care or who are at risk or in trouble with the law

✦ children who have problems at school (e.g. chronic absenteeism).

The Social Worker can work as part of a public service organisation (e.g. local council, care and education team), but many private organisations also employ Social Workers. The Social Worker usually has responsibility for a number of children and works individually with each of them, with the parents, other family members and with the childcare and education setting, as appropriate.

Evaluation

Each child is evaluated individually by means of information questionnaires, checklists, interviews with the child and others involved; and input is often sought from allied professionals (e.g. a Child Psychologist, a medical doctor).

The Social Worker can provide information about facilities, and arrange appropriate support and care services, as well as follow-up referrals, appointments and therapy programmes.

Further information

Joseph Rowntree Foundation, www.jrf.org.uk (funds and publishes research projects into various social welfare issues) (accessed 20 September 2005)

►► Speech and Language Therapists

Speech and Language Therapists work to assess, diagnose and develop a programme to maximise the communication potential of the people referred to them. In some countries (e.g. the USA) the profession refers to a Speech and Language Pathologist (SLP).

Speech and Language Therapists typically evaluate children referred for a range of *LANGUAGE AND SPEECH* **disorder**s and difficulties; for example:

✦ *AUTISM* and other disorders with social interaction difficulties
✦ feeding and swallowing difficulties
✦ *HEARING* loss
✦ language delay
✦ physical **impairment**
✦ specific difficulties in producing sounds (e.g. a child with a *CLEFT LIP AND PALATE*, a lisp)
✦ specific language impairment
✦ *STUTTERING/STAMMERING/*dysfluency.

The Speech and Language Therapist can work individually with a child, carrying out an assessment, then planning and implementing a programme that focuses on the specific skills identified in the evaluation. The Speech and Language Therapist can also work as a consultant, educating parents and others about the reasons for the child's difficulties, and demonstrating how to work with the child and how to help the child apply skills learned in individual therapy sessions to the mainstream setting. Speech and Language Therapists work in health centres, nurseries, schools, rehabilitation centres and in the home, and can work in public or private practice, or both.

Evaluation

Typically, the Speech and Language Therapist gathers information from parents and from significant others working with the child and carries out a variety of activities in individual sessions with the child. The Speech and Language Therapist evaluates the range of communication skills (i.e. **oro-motor** functioning, phonology, receptive and expressive language, word retrieval skills, syntax and grammar, pragmatic and semantic skills), as well as the child's ability to plan, organise and attend to details (**executive function**).

175

The Speech and Language Therapist plans and implements a therapy programme based on the assessment findings and can also suggest activities, toys and games that can be used at the day-care centre, at school and at home.

The Speech and Language Therapist may also recommend assessment by allied professionals (e.g. *OCCUPATIONAL THERAPIST*, *EDUCATIONAL PSYCHOLOGIST*, **neurologist**).

Further information

Royal College of Speech and Language Therapists, www.rcslt.org (accessed 20 September 2005)

➤➤ Steiner (Waldorf-Steiner) education

Rudolf Steiner believed that education should be designed to meet the changing needs of children as they develop physically, mentally and emotionally, not to meet the goals desired by adults or by society in general.

Background

Steiner was born in 1861 and was a gifted academic. Early in adult life he became involved in anthroposophy and spiritual science, philosophies based on the belief that religious life (any religion), science, culture, politics and economics should be in balance, with none of them dominating our lives. He was also involved in the development of homeopathy.

The term Waldorf-Steiner originated from Steiner's first school, which was financed by the owner of the Waldorf Astoria cigarette factory, who asked Steiner to set up a school for employees' children.

At the time, Steiner's ideas were quite popular and his schools were well funded, but from the 1930s to the 1960s, his ideas were considered impractical and too 'spiritual'. In recent years, however, there has been renewed interest in his holistic approach to life, health and education.

Key points

✦ To age 7: encourage play, drawing, storytelling, home-schooling, nature study.

✦ Do not teach children younger than 7 to read.

✦ Teach a child to write before you teach them to read.

✦ Allow one teacher to teach the same class for 7 years.

✦ Allow children to concentrate on one subject at a time (e.g. history for 2 hours per day for several weeks, then geography for 2 hours per day, etc.).

✦ Find links between art and science.

✦ Interact with children to foster enthusiasm for the material being covered.

✦ Give a moral lead, but do not teach a particular set of beliefs.

✦ Encourage learning for its own sake, rather than for taking exams.

Modern Steiner schools

There are several hundred Steiner (or Waldorf) schools throughout the world, although over time different Steiner schools located in different parts of the world have developed different characteristics. Some are more faithful to the original Steiner model, while others have modified the Steiner curriculum, sometimes in order to receive government funding.

Some Steiner schools today are also considered New Age (a term describing a wide-ranging set of beliefs and practices, including personal spiritual growth, self-realisation and holistic medicine). The home-schooling movement also reflects many of Steiner's principles and concepts.

Further information

Steiner Education, www.freedom-in-education.co.uk/steiner.htm (accessed 20 September 2005)

The Steiner Waldorf Schools' Fellowship, www.steinerwaldorf.org.uk (accessed 20 September 2005)

➤➤ Stuttering/stammering

Stuttering (dysfluency) occurs when the flow of speech is interrupted by abnormal repetitions and prolongations (drawing out) of sounds, syllables, words or phrases, often accompanied by struggle behaviours (trying to force the sound/word out or gain extra time by swallowing, blinking, face muscle contortions, and so on).

Causes

✦ Genetic: research shows that stuttering tends to occur in families; more boys stutter than girls.

✦ Organic: there is some evidence of certain brain abnormalities in people who stutter; these abnormalities are detected only when the individual is speaking.

Theories

Learning theory

Children learn to stutter during the language development process.

✦ Language emerges and the child tries to compose messages with the right words.

✦ When nervous or excited, the child becomes dysfluent and receives a negative reaction (e.g. 'Slow down').

✦ Struggle behaviours develop and the child receives a negative reaction to them.

✦ **Anxiety** increases and this causes increased stuttering.

Psychological theory

Stuttering is a symptom of emotional upset and *PSYCHOTHERAPY* is needed.

Normal dysfluency versus stuttering

✦ Most children are dysfluent between 2 and 5 years of age.

✦ With normal dysfluency there are no struggle behaviours.

✦ Non-stutterers tend to struggle with whole words and phrases; stutterers struggle more with sounds and syllables.

✦ Dysfluency in non-stutterers is inconsistent, but frequent in stutterers.

✦ Non-stutterers do not show tension when dysfluent, but stutterers do.

Treatment

The key is early detection. Approximately 85 per cent of children who begin stuttering as pre-schoolers outgrow it before adolescence, but it is important to have a speech evaluation at the onset of the dysfluency, especially where there is a family history of stuttering. A properly qualified and experienced *SPEECH AND LANGUAGE THERAPIST* should carry out the initial evaluation. Further referrals may be made to other professionals (e.g. a **neurologist**).

There tend to be two approaches to treatment:
+ fluency (zero stuttering): teach the stutterer to speak all over again, from scratch (not considered particularly successful)
+ modification: to stutter with ease and help the child overcome the fear of stuttering.

In general, *do not*:
+ imply that stuttering is a bad habit
+ tell the stutterer to stop and start over, to stop and think
+ help with words (wait for the child to speak independently)
+ tell him/her to talk slower/faster, in a low/high voice, to swallow, to take a deep breath, and so on
+ call attention to the stuttering if s/he is unaware of it
+ make the child compete for a chance to talk (e.g. circle-time)
+ make the child compete in verbal activities (e.g. flashcard drill).

Further information

Ability, www.ability.org.uk/stuttering.html (accessed 20 September 2005)

➤➤ Temperament and personality

Temperament

There are a number of models that describe temperament (e.g. type theory, trait theory); a traits model is presented here.

Under this model, temperament is a set of traits that helps us to organise our approach to the world. These traits appear to be relatively stable from birth. They are not particularly good/bad or right/wrong, just more or less of something (e.g. some children are noisier than others, some are more cuddly, some have more regular sleep patterns, and so on).

Understanding a child's temperament can help to anticipate issues that might present difficulties, and knowing a child's temperament can also help decide whether a behaviour is a problem or whether it just needs to be handled differently. Temperament is not an excuse for bad behaviour, however, or for overlooking a genuine difficulty in adapting and coping.

Temperament traits (from Doctors Chess and Thomas)

✦ Activity level is the child's 'motor' speed. Is the child:

   a   a wriggler and squirmer or one who sits and quietly watches?

   b   always on the go or happier with quieter, less energetic activities?

✦ Distractibility is the level of concentration and attention, especially when the child is not particularly interested in an activity. Easy distractibility is positive when it is easy to divert a child from an undesirable behaviour, but negative when it means the child finds it difficult to finish tasks. Is the child:

   a   easily distracted by sounds or sights?

   b   easily calmed with an alternate activity?

✦ Intensity is the force of a response, be it positive or negative. Does the child:

   a   react strongly and loudly to everything, even relatively small things?

   b   show dramatic pleasure or upset, or get quiet when upset?

✦ Regularity refers to ease or acceptance of routines. Is the child:

   a   predictable or unpredictable/accepting or resistant (e.g. in sleep patterns, meal-times, toileting)?

✦ Sensory threshold is how much stimulation it takes to produce a response in the child. Does the child:

   a   react positively or negatively to particular sounds, textures, smells, tastes?

   b   startle easily/react slowly or vaguely?

   c   feel the heat easily?

✦ Approach/withdrawal is the characteristic response to a new situation or strangers. Does the child:

a   eagerly approach new situations or people?

b   seem hesitant or resistant with new situations, people or things?

✦ Adaptability is how easily the child adapts to transitions (e.g. changing to a new activity, changing a routine). Does the child:

a   fit in easily, 'jump in' with enthusiasm?

b   take a long time to become comfortable?

✦ Persistence is how long a child can keep going even when something is difficult. Does the child:

a   continue to work on a difficult puzzle or quickly move on to another activity?

b   wait quietly to have needs met or demand loudly?

c   react crossly when asked to stop an activity?

✦ Mood is the tendency towards optimism or pessimism. Does the child:

a   generally demonstrate a happy or a serious mood?

b   generally look forward to things or predict, 'It's not going to be fun', or 'I won't win'.

Personality

Different ideas also surround the idea of personality, what it is, how it is measured, and so on.

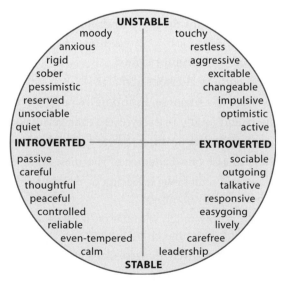

Fig 31 ▲ A model of personality types based on the theory of H. J. Eysenck

Doctors Chess and Thomas suggest that personality is the interaction between temperament and environment – our preferences for where and how we like to work, play, relax, and so on. It is not a hard-and-fast mould we are forced into, but a set of tendencies.

Personality types

Theoretical models of personality types often use certain descriptive words grouped into basic categories. One of the most famous models is that of Eysenck. It groups traits on two intersecting lines – 'Stable' to 'Unstable' on the vertical, and 'Introverted' to 'Extroverted' on the horizontal (see figure 31).

'Managing' a child's temperament and personality

Being 'temperamental' is not necessarily negative and does not apply only to impulsive, dramatic outbursts; having an exuberant or a quiet personality is not necessarily a problem. Sometimes, however, personalities may need 'managing'.

✦ Get to know the child's temperament and personality and plan ahead for troublesome, or potentially troublesome, behaviour; for example, if the child tends to get overexcited on special occasions, step in before it gets out of hand (keep the occasion short, take the child aside to break the cycle).

✦ Step back and try to determine the reasons for a behaviour. For example, if a high-energy child knocks another child over, was it a mistake or deliberate? Either way he was wrong, but the punishment should fit the 'crime'. In the first case the child should at least say sorry and then be helped to work off energy in a more suitable space; in the second the child might have to lose a special privilege to reinforce the consequences of deliberately hurting someone else.

✦ Structure routines for a child who is not good at them (e.g. toileting).

✦ Intersperse high-focus activities with soothing activities (e.g. water-play, story-time).

✦ Help children recognise and name their own temperament and their own problem signs.

✦ Explain what they could do to feel better if they feel 'like that'.

✦ Avoid reacting intensely yourself; give calm, clear suggestions or directions.

✦ Talk about changes and plans ahead of time.

✦ Finish an activity a few minutes earlier to allow time for tidying up in a calm way.

✦ Build in extra time for slow-to-react or methodical children to finish an activity.

➤➤ Testing children: Psycho-educational evaluation

This entry is headed 'testing' because it is the word so often used to describe some form of professional evaluation carried out when parents or others are concerned about a child's skills, progress, development or behaviour.

Psycho-educational evaluation looks at a child's performance (usually compared to his/her peers) on a number of tasks and skills, and at how a child thinks, reasons, and so on. It can consider overall development, behaviour, learning **aptitude** and specific developmental aspects (e.g. language). In early-years and school settings, evaluations are often coordinated by *EDUCATIONAL PSYCHOLOGISTS*, with input from others as appropriate (e.g. *SPEECH AND LANGUAGE THERAPISTS, OCCUPATIONAL THERAPISTS*).

Evaluation usually consists of a battery (group) of tests. Tests can be subjective and objective; they should always be administered by a person with appropriate training and/or qualifications, and a confidential written report should be provided.

Subjective assessment tools

These use personal opinion and recollection and, as such, they are open to bias and inaccuracies. This does not mean that they are useless, only that they have to be recognised for what they are. Examples include:

✦ personal reports
✦ questionnaires used to collect information (e.g. about family history, behaviour)
✦ checklists (e.g. of developmental milestones)
✦ rating scales (e.g. of behaviour, likes/dislikes).

Objective/standardised assessment tools

These are designed to be scored/rated without personal judgement. They are **standardised** using a set of strict guidelines that compare an individual child's response to the responses of other children of about the same age and with a similar mix of various factors (e.g. ethnic background, socio-economic status). They use techniques such as **statistics** to make them as reliable as possible. Standardised tools can include:

✦ multiple-choice tests
✦ **IQ tests**
✦ rating scales (e.g. behaviour, feelings)

✦ checklists

✦ specific diagnostic tests (e.g. speech and/or language)

✦ tests of **achievement** of particular skills (e.g. reading, spelling).

Assessment battery

This is a combination of tools used to collect as much information as possible in order to make a thorough assessment of the situation.

Examiner qualifications

These are the qualifications needed before a person can legally administer tests. Some tests do not require specific qualifications or training. However, even then it should be ensured that the person giving a test understands it and knows how to administer it, interpret it and use the findings for the benefit of the child.

Confidentiality

Confidentiality is essential when evaluating children and presenting findings and recommendations. A written report should detail the reasons for evaluation, the methods used, the findings and the conclusions.

➤➤ Testing children: Standardisation

Standardised (objective) tests use a sample of children to establish a type of average or **norm** and then compare other children against that norm. This creates some problems for fairness, since not all children come from the same kind of background and opportunity (e.g. language, culture, socio-economic), and one could end up comparing apples and oranges as if they were one and the same thing.

However, most tests try to take all this into account so as not to allow unfair comparisons. Some English-language tests have been translated into other languages (but that does not always make the content 'culture-fair'); and some tests use samples of children from different countries to make the test more reliable for all children of those countries. In addition, test samples try to include children from all sorts of backgrounds, geographical areas, and so on.

In fact, most tests are developed very carefully, and **statistics** are used to standardise them and to make it very clear what comparisons can reliably be made.

Standardising procedures

Each test comes with information about how the test was developed, what types of children were used as a sample for comparisons, what the norms are, a set of instructions about what materials are needed, where the child/children should be tested and specific guidelines about what the administrator of the test should say, how to mark the test and how to interpret results.

In addition, all scores include a chance factor (called 'probability'), because it is impossible to control for every little thing (e.g. maybe the child made a number of lucky guesses), and within agreed limits this chance factor is acceptable.

Standardised procedures aim to ensure that every time the test is administered, each child or group experiences the same conditions, and that good/bad/indifferent results are most likely the result of the ability, knowledge or skill that the test is supposed to be measuring.

Norms

Before a test is used for actual evaluation purposes, it is tried out on as many children as possible, who are grouped according to as many things as possible that might influence their performance (e.g. age, gender, ethnicity, family income). This is the normative sample.

These sample scores are then sorted into most common to least common scores. They are then said to be typical of what most children of a particular age, ethnicity, and so on, would probably score (the norm).

The idea is that about 70 per cent of any group performing on the same task will probably score about the same (which becomes the average or mean); 15 per cent will score somewhere higher; and 15 per cent somewhere lower. This is called the normal distribution (see figure 32).

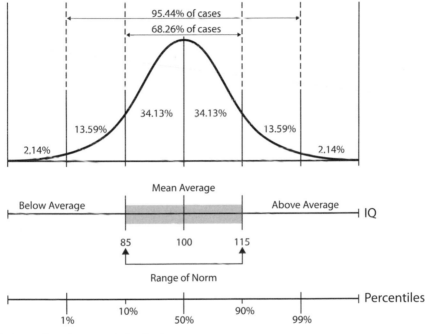

Fig 32 ▲ Simple normal distribution curve

Actual scores (raw scores) are then converted to standardised measures by statistical methods, and are included in the test manual to help decide what the test results really mean.

Standardised measures

These include age norms, standard scores, percentiles and stanines, with standard scores probably being the most reported.

✦ Age norms describe the ages when most of the children in the normative sample demonstrate particular skills or sets of skills. Norm ages are never a set year and month, but an age range, to take into account developmental differences and/or the fact that chance may have played a small part in the child's scores. So, when a child's actual/raw score on a reading ability test converts to a Reading Age of 7 years 2 months (± 6 months), it means that the child shows the skills most typical of children aged between 6 years 8 months and 7 years 8 months). If the child's actual age is 7 years, then s/he fits within the norm. If the child's actual age is 8 years 6 months, however, then the child has skills more typical of a child who is younger, and questions should be asked about why this is so, and what can be done about it.

✦ Standard Scores use the average score (norm) obtained by the sample, and call it 100. As with age norms, Standard Scores allow for some error and build in a range of the average (usually 100 ± 15). Children who score higher than 115 are then considered to be performing above average and those below 85 are below average, on whatever skill, trait or **aptitude** is being measured.

✦ Stanines use a scale of 1–9 and function in the same way as the other standardised measures.

✦ Percentiles are numbered from 0–100 per cent, with the 50th percentile being the norm. A percentile of 50 means that 50 per cent of children of similar background (age, ethnicity, etc.) could be expected to do the same as, or better than, the child being tested, and 50 per cent would do the same or worse. Thus, a percentile of 20 per cent means that 80 per cent of similar children would do the same or better and that the child being tested is in the lowest 20 per cent (for age, gender or whatever factors are included in the normative sample). A percentile does not refer to the percentage of questions answered correctly or incorrectly.

Further information

Hayes, N. and Stratton, P., *A Student's Dictionary of Psychology*, 4th edn, Hodder Arnold, London, 2003.

➤➤ Testing children: Types of tests

Achievement/competency tests

These measure what a child knows/can do at a given point in time with regard to a specific set of skills (e.g. reading, mathematics, PE skills). Results can place the child alongside his actual peer group (e.g. class) or alongside a wider **norm**.

No specific qualifications are usually required to administer these tests.

Examples include: Schonell Graded Word Reading and Spelling, Wide-Range Achievement Tests.

Checklists/rating scales

These ask people (e.g. parents, teachers, early-years workers, sometimes the child) to rate certain behaviours, feelings, and so on. Others ask an observer to check off behaviours/skills seen and to rate their quality or frequency.

Trained professionals should administer and interpret such tests.

Examples include: Connors Behaviour Rating Scale, Bayley Scales of Infant Development, Portage Checklist, Movement Assessment Battery.

IQ (intelligence quotient) tests

These describe the measured relationship between a child's actual age and mental age (**intelligence**). They measure the child's **aptitude** for learning, not current **achievement** or competency.

The norm is assumed to be 100, with a range of ± 15. A score above 115 is considered above average (with extended ratings, such as superior and including the gifted range) and a score below 85 to be below average (with certain points denoting degree of **intellectual impairment**).

Some tests provide both verbal and non-verbal scores, some a single 'global' IQ and yet others non-verbal scores only. They measure **cognition**s such as verbal comprehension, visual spatial thinking and memory.

Special qualifications are required to administer these tests (e.g. *EDUCATIONAL PSYCHOLOGISTS*, neuro-psychologists).

Examples include: Wechsler Intelligence Scale for Children (WISC), Stanford-Binet Intelligence Scale, Raven's Progressive Matrices.

Specific skills, abilities and aptitude tests

These are used by specialists such as Educational Psychologists, SPEECH AND LANGUAGE THERAPISTS and *OCCUPATIONAL THERAPISTS*. They are usually **standardised** and provide information about specific skills, such as visual-spatial organisation, vocabulary, articulation, fine- and gross-motor skills, muscle tone, and so on.

Special qualifications are needed to administer and interpret them.

Examples include: Bender Visual Motor Gestalt Test, Peabody Picture Vocabulary Scale, Preschool Clinical Evaluation of Language Fundamentals (P-CELF).

Information-processing (perceptual) skills tests

These look closely at specific abilities, such as the ability to remember series of letters, to clearly hear sounds or to detect rhyming words. They are particularly useful when trying to understand exactly where a child is having difficulties with school tasks.

Trained care and education workers and other professionals are able to administer many of these tests without additional qualifications.

Examples include: Phonological Assessment Battery (PhaB), The Listening Skills Test, Test of Auditory Analysis Skills (TAAS), the Developmental Test of Visual Perception.

➤➤ Tomatis method

Also called auditory training, auditory stimulation and listening therapy, the Tomatis method claims to benefit a wide variety of **disorder**s (e.g. *DYSLEXIA, ATTENTION DEFICIT DISORDERS (ADD), AUTISM*). Independent research indicates that Tomatis principles are plausible, but there is no conclusion as yet about the method's scientific validity, and personal experiences reported by parents vary considerably.

The method, named after its founder, states that:

✦ The ear integrates/puts together *all* the sensory information (not just what is heard) that the body receives.

✦ Listening is the key to learning, and listening problems are caused by a sensory regulation problem that begins in the inner ear.

✦ If the ear does not function properly, the brain cannot send out appropriate instructions to the body.

✦ The ear can be trained to listen effectively.

✦ People have a dominant ear, with right-ear dominance best for efficient learning.

✦ Listening and communication begins in the womb.

Principles

✦ Good hearing is the foundation of good listening.

✦ To be a good learner, one has to be a good listener.

✦ Good listeners can filter information (focus on/select what is important).

✦ The inner ear controls balance, coordination, muscle tone and every single muscle in our body, including the muscles of our eyes.

✦ Sound is conducted through air and bone (the 'other' ear). Sound conducted through air and bone must be in the right balance, with air conduction being dominant.

✦ People who are right-ear dominant learn more easily and are better able to control speech and voice intensity, frequency, timbre, rhythm and sentence flow.

Method

Programmes are custom-made but follow a basic pattern using the Electronic Ear, a tape recorder where sound is filtered and frequency adjusted.

+ Initially, sessions consist of listening to very high frequencies similar to prenatal sounds, which reproduce the auditory stages of development, the idea being that this re-teaches the listening process and makes it possible to switch ear dominance from left to right.

+ The special headphone is equipped with a vibrator (for bone and ear listening), and over time ear listening becomes dominant.

+ Passive exercises are gradually combined with active exercises utilising the voice. Then active listening therapy and microphone work are included, to further improve the ear-brain-voice connection.

Further information

Tomatis, www.tomatis.com (accessed 20 September 2005)

►► Tonsils

The tonsils are two clumps of tissue on each side of the back of the mouth, near the throat. They are made up of lymphocyte tissue. Lymphocytes are involved in the production of **antibodies** (which help the body to fight *INFECTIONS*). However, there seems to be no adverse effect on health when the tonsils are removed.

It is thought that perhaps the tonsils were not designed to effectively handle the viral infections that occur in children in a modern urban population. It may also be that the tonsils were more important in dealing with certain types of infections (e.g. worms, other parasites) that are now relatively uncommon.

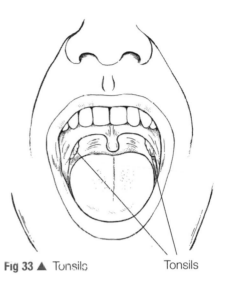

Fig 33 ▲ Tonsils   Tonsils

Tonsillitis

Sometimes the tonsils become problematic (e.g. tonsillitis). Symptoms include:

+ red, swollen tonsils that may have a white or yellow coating
+ sore throat
+ pain or discomfort when swallowing
+ *FEVER*
+ raspy voice
+ swollen glands in the neck.

Treatment

Recurrent sore throats and infections should be checked by a doctor, who should also check for strep throat (Streptococcus A infection, a bacteria that causes excess mucus). Because of success with *ANTIBIOTICS*, surgery is no longer the standard treatment for tonsillitis. However, a tonsillectomy could well be recommended if the child has:

+ persistent or recurrent tonsillitis
+ recurrent sore throats
+ recurrent throat infections

+ swollen tonsils that make it hard to breathe
+ difficulty swallowing
+ obstructive sleep apnoea (the child stops breathing for a few seconds at a time during sleep, because enlarged tonsils partially block the airway).

If surgery is recommended, during the tonsillectomy:

+ the child has a general anaesthetic (in an operating room, with an anaesthetist present)
+ the child is asleep for about 20 minutes
+ the surgeon reaches the tonsils through the child's open mouth – there is no skin incision
+ the tonsils are removed by incision and the blood vessels are cauterised (sealed).

An intracapsular tonsillectomy is a variation on this more traditional approach. Obstructing tissue is removed, but a small layer of tonsil tissue is left in place to protect the underlying throat muscles. Recovery is usually faster because there is less pain and less medication, and eating and drinking are more comfortable.

Further information

KidsHealth, www.kidshealth.com (accessed 20 September 2005)

Patient UK, www.patient.co.uk/showdoc/40024904 (accessed 20 September 2005)

➤➤ Twins/multiple birth siblings

Twins can be identical or fraternal and can occur in multiple births of more than two siblings (e.g. triplets with two identical siblings and one fraternal). UK **statistics** indicate that multiple births have increased by 20 per cent in the last 10 years.

Identical versus fraternal

Identical (monozygotic/uniovular) twins develop from a single egg/sperm combination that splits a few days after conception. Their **DNA** originates from a single source, so **genetic** characteristics are similar. However, the idea that identical twins are exactly alike is not quite true, since sometimes there are birth differences that remain (e.g. weight differences), and some differences emerge over time (e.g. interests, academic success).

Fraternal (dizygotic/biovular) multiples form when 2 separate eggs are fertilised by separate sperm at the same time. Apart from age, they are no more alike than any other siblings might be, sharing about 50 per cent of their genetic characteristics.

Care and education settings

When multiple birth siblings start day-care, school, and so on, certain issues present themselves; for example: whether to separate them or not, and, if so, at what age this should take place. There are also many misconceptions and opinions, such as:

✦ multiple birth siblings, particularly if they are identical, should be separated/kept together

✦ multiple birth siblings are always the best of friends/in competition with each other

✦ one of the siblings is always a leader/stronger/more social and will dominate the other/s.

Separation

This is a decision that should consider:

✦ the parents' opinion, knowledge of their children and preference

✦ the siblings' behaviour when they are together/apart

✦ the overdependency of one sibling on another/the others (not always an argument for separation, since it could be quite traumatic)

✦ the interdependency of the siblings (same argument as above)

✦ individual interests, abilities and the early-years and school settings available.

195

Working with multiple-birth siblings

The following may seem obvious, but it serves as a reminder against assumptions.

✦ Talk first with the parents about each child's interests, behaviours and personality, and about the relationships at home.

✦ Get to know and encourage each child's interests, abilities, and so on, and manage them individually.

✦ Avoid talking about the siblings as 'the twins' or 'the triplets'. Use their individual names, remembering first and last names when marking off a list or register (e.g. Carly Jones, Rachel Jones, rather than Carly and Rachel Jones).

✦ When multiple siblings are involved in group naughtiness, do not assume equal guilt. Reward/punish on the same basis as you would any of the other children involved.

Further information

Twins and Multiple Births Association (TAMBA), www.tamba.org.uk (accessed 20 September 2005)

➤➤ Vision: How we see

The eye is a small ball held in the eye socket by muscles (figure 34). Light enters the eye through the cornea, a transparent layer of tissue. The cornea bends the light rays through the pupil, which is the dark, round opening in the centre of the iris (which gives us eye colour). The light then reaches the lens, immediately behind the pupil. More delicate adjustments are made to the path of the light rays to focus them on the retina, the membrane that

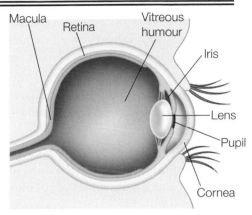

Fig 34 ▲ The eye

lines the inside back wall of the eye. It contains nerve cells which change the light rays into electrical impulses that are then sent via the optic nerve to the brain, where an image is perceived.

Vision tests

Children should have their first eye exam by about 4 years of age and then a check-up every 2–3 years.

An eye examination should check:
+ normal muscle movement
+ peripheral vision (the ability to see out of the side of the eyes)
+ internal structures of the eye
+ defects or scratches on the surface of the front of the eye (cornea)
+ the pressure inside the eye (test for glaucoma)
+ visual acuity of each eye: reading a standard eye chart, 20/20 vision = excellent vision (the larger the bottom number of the fraction, the worse the vision)
+ the ability to distinguish colours (e.g. Ishihara Test for Colour Blindness).

'Normal' test results are as follows:
+ 20/20 vision
+ the ability to correctly identify colours
+ normal optic nerve, retina, blood vessels and back of the eyeball
+ no evidence of glaucoma
+ a transparent cornea, free of scratches.

Vision care professionals

✦ Ophthalmologist: a medical doctor who has specialised in vision and eye diseases, who can write medical prescriptions and prescriptions for corrective lenses (glasses, contact lenses) and who can perform surgery on the eye.

✦ Optometrist: a professional trained in vision and eye diseases, who can prescribe corrective lenses and diagnose eye diseases, but who does not perform surgery.

✦ Optician: a professional who makes and fits corrective lenses.

✦ Orthoptist: a professional trained in the diagnosis and treatment of vision and abnormalities of eye movement and eye position (e.g. lazy eye).

➤➤ Vision: Childhood disorders, diseases and impairment

Disorders and diseases

+ Strabismus: misalignment of the eyes, causing two images to be sent to the brain instead of one.
+ Refractive disorders: the cornea and lens do not work well together, causing: short-sight (myopia); far-sight (hyperopia); astigmatism (inability to focus on just one point); and anisometropia (the two eyes do not focus equally).
+ Amblyopia: loss of vision due to abnormal **neuron** development (often the result of untreated strabismus).
+ Congenital cataracts: opacity (milkiness) of the lens, causing blurred vision.
+ Paediatric glaucoma: high fluid pressure in the eye, causing optic nerve damage and vision loss.
+ Retinopathy immaturity: the immature eye is damaged by exposure to high concentrations of oxygen (e.g. in premature birth).

Impairment

Visual **impairment** is loss of vision, due to a **disorder** or a disease.

+ Partially sighted: sighted children who have special educational needs as a result of impairment.
+ Low vision: sighted children who are unable to read newspaper-type print at normal viewing distance, even with eyeglasses/contact lenses. **Multi-sensory** learning, modifications to lighting and size of print, and sometimes Braille are needed.
+ Legally blind: children with less than 20/200 vision in the better eye, or a very limited field of vision (20 degrees at its widest point). Braille or other non-visual media are needed for learning.

Symptoms of vision problems

Symptoms may include the following:
+ eyes shake, wander randomly
+ eyes do not follow the carer's face
+ excessively large or small pupils
+ pupils are not black and appear cloudy

◆ eyes cross or turn outward
◆ squinting
◆ frequent eye-rubbing
◆ complaints of tired eyes
◆ better day than night vision
◆ the child does not seem to focus
◆ the child turns/tilts head, covers/closes an eye when looking at detail
◆ the child avoids close-up work or tires quickly on such tasks
◆ the child seems to be clumsy.

Treatment/rehabilitation

◆ Functional vision exam: to determine the extent of a person's remaining sight and what treatment or rehabilitation is required/possible.
◆ Rehabilitation: to maintain or regain independence after loss of vision.
◆ Counselling: to address emotional needs and problems.
◆ Adaptive/assistive technology: e.g. magnification, lighting to maximise remaining sight.
◆ Optical aids: e.g. bi-optic glasses, computer software.
◆ Non-optical aids: e.g. talking calculators and watches, large-print calendars.
◆ Independent living skills: e.g. cooking, dressing.
◆ Orientation/mobility training: e.g. safety skills, independent travel skills at home, at school.

Further information

The National Federation of Families with Visually Impaired Children, www.look-uk.org (accessed 20 September 2005)

Patient UK, www.patient.co.uk/showdoc/40024572 (accessed 20 September 2005)

►► Vision: Colour blindness/deficiency

Normally, people can accurately see and match all colours of the spectrum by mixtures of the three basic colour sensitivities (red, green, blue), but colour blind people cannot do this. The **disorder** is more common in males and is most often due to an inherited **chromosomal** condition.

Colour blindness is really a deficiency and virtually no one is truly blind to all colours.

+ Red-weakness (protanomaly): redness is weaker in depth and brightness, and colours seem paler (e.g. the redness in violet is weakened and only blue is seen) and shifted towards green.
+ Green-weakness (deuteranomaly): small differences in the red, orange, yellow and green regions of the spectrum seem more red; it is also difficult to distinguish violet from blue.
+ Combination (dicromasy): red, orange, yellow and green all appear to be the same.

Diagnosis

Colour deficiency is diagnosed through clinical *TESTING* (e.g. Ishihara Test). There is no treatment, and although it can make some things frustrating and/or dangerous, most colour-deficient people compensate well.

Problems

+ Buying clothes: poor colour combinations and choices (a 'disaster' at the age when children want to choose their own clothes).
+ Chemical tests: interpreting chemical tests (e.g. litmus paper turned red by acid).
+ Cooking and foods: is it tomato sauce or chocolate syrup? Some food can look disgusting (it is not surprising some children think spinach is 'yukky').
+ Kids and crayons (e.g. when choosing blue to colour the ocean).
+ LEDs (the lights that glow on devices such as TVs): is the light red, yellow or green? Is it on or off?
+ Map/graph reading: colour codes/keys/legends.
+ Teacher's helper: she asked me to get the red book on her desk, but which one is red?
+ Team games: my team's wearing green shirts, but which are the green shirts?

+ Traffic lights: not a problem if they use standard colour order and position (red, yellow, green running top to bottom) and the child knows the order.

How to help

+ Ask a classmate to help when tasks need colour recognition (e.g. put all the red shapes in the red box).
+ Give children an idea of what a colour looks like from their perspective (e.g. green looks a bit like brown).
+ Have children's eyes tested before teaching colours.
+ Label coloured pencils, pens, etc. with their colour word.
+ Label pictures with words or symbols if colour recognition is needed.
+ Photocopy material printed with coloured ink on to white paper.
+ Use white markers on blackboards (and black on white) to maximise contrast, and avoid yellow or orange on green boards.

Further information

Medicdirect, www.medicdirect.co.uk/clinics (click on 'Eyes', then select 'Colour blindness') (accessed 20 September)

Ishihara Test for Colour Blindness, www.toledo-bend.com/colorblind/Ishihara.html (accessed 20 September 2005)

Glossary

ability: a skill, a capacity to be able to do something.

abstract: activities, ideas, thoughts that do not need actual (concrete) materials in order to be understood.

achievement: successfully reaching a target or goal, acquiring a new skill.

acupuncture: a treatment which can relieve symptoms of some physical and psychological conditions. Typically, fine needles are inserted through the skin and left in position briefly, sometimes with manual or electrical stimulation.

allergen: a substance which is not necessarily harmful in itself, but which produces a response from the **immune system**, causing symptoms ranging from mild discomfort (e.g. sneezing, watery eyes) to potentially life threatening (e.g. anaphylactic shock).

antibodies: substances in the body that react to allergens and produce allergic symptoms.

anxiety: excessive unhappiness, worry, fear, often to the point where it interferes with usual patterns of behaviour.

applied behaviour analysis (ABA): a strategy for teaching specific skills using a combination of behaviourism, behaviour management strategies and a careful analysis of what the person's current skill levels are and how to take them on to the next step. It is frequently used to help children with **disorders** such as Autism and Down's **Syndrome**.

aptitude: how easy/difficult it will be for a person to learn a new skill or reach a target or goal.

body image: a person's idea of their body, both physically and in the 'eyes' of other people. It involves a sense of where the body parts are, how they move, body shape and 'attractiveness'.

brain scans: different ways of measuring brain activity and functioning, including **EEG, CAT, PET, MRI, FMRI** and **MEG** scans. (The initials often indicate the technology involved, e.g. MRI = magnetic resonance imaging.)

chromosomal abnormalities: an unusual characteristic of any of the 46 chromosomes each person normally carries (e.g. a piece missing, an extra piece added on).

chromosomes: 'structures' that exist inside cells in the body which carry **DNA** (compounds which carry **genetic** information).

cognition: mental activities that include thinking, reasoning, memory and concepts.

cortico-steroid: there are two separate but related definitions:

✦ **cortico-steroid drug**: drug that suppresses the **immune system** and thereby interferes with inflammatory overreaction. Hence 'anti-inflammatory' drugs.

✦ **cortico-steroid hormone**: produced by the adrenal gland (which is involved in metabolism/energy levels).

cortisone: synthetic (manufactured/artificial) **steroid**.

decoding: the process of breaking down whole words into their individual letter sounds or sound combinations and matching them to letter symbols in order to be able to read/write them (e.g. cat = c-a-t, shout = sh-ou-t). It relies on a good knowledge of letter symbols and their matching sounds, knowledge of the rules of sound units (e.g. o + u = 'ou', as in shout) and contextual clues (e.g. a clue from a picture might confirm that the word really does say 'cat'). It is the reverse of **encoding**.

developmental stages (ages/expectations): broad time periods in a child's development and growth that define when we can expect to see certain skills, behaviours, and so on.

Diagnostic and Statistical Manual (DSM-IV): a publication of the American Psychiatric Association used by many physicians, psychiatrists and psychologists, particularly in the USA, for diagnosis of various behavioural **syndrome**s and **disorder**s.

disorder: disturbance of regular functioning (body, brain, language, etc.).

DNA: compounds found in **chromosomes** and containing **genetic** codes for the various characteristics we inherit from our parents' genetic make-up (e.g. eye colour, hair colour).

Doctors Chess and Thomas: researchers into child development, particularly the factors that determine and/or influence the development of temperament and personality (see *TEMPERAMENT TRAITS AND PERSONALITY TYPES*).

dysgraphia: a handwriting **disorder** (see *HANDWRITING*).

ear infections: middle or inner ear infections, with middle ear infections the most common (see *MIDDLE EAR INFECTIONS, HEARING, INFECTIONS*).

EEG (electroencephalogram): a recording of the naturally produced electrical signals of the brain during different states (e.g. asleep, awake, anaesthetised), showing any abnormalities as well as how long it takes the brain to process various stimuli.

egocentricity: described in Piaget's theory of child development, and typical of the child aged from birth through to about six years of age. The child sees and understands the world only through his/her own eyes and believes others see things the same way.

encoding: the reverse process of **decoding**. It is sometimes referred to as 'blending'.

executive function: functions within the brain that activate, organise, integrate and manage other functions (e.g. the memory pulls together all the relevant bits of information available to help us solve a problem).

failure to thrive: poor growth in infants and young children (the lowest 3 per cent for children of that age, sex, population) as a result of insufficient nutrition due to physical factors (e.g. medical **disorder**) or environmental factors (e.g. neglect).

genetic(s): genetics is the study of genes, which are carried by **chromosomes** and determine inherited (genetic) characteristics (e.g. colour of eyes).

global intelligence: the idea that **intelligence** is a single, 'general' measure and is not directly determined or explained by any particular **ability** (e.g. verbal/non-verbal).

horizontal palmar grasp: an immature grasp of a pencil, crayon, etc. The child grasps the utensil in his/her fist, and draws/writes with the fist horizontal to the surface he/she is working on.

immaturity: indicates delay in development, causing problems that, with time, may be overcome. However, delay can affect the quality of a skill as it develops, and time alone often is not enough.

immune system: reacts to any threat (e.g. **allergens**, a skin irritation) to the body's physiological functioning by producing **antibodies** (protein) to attack the threat. This triggers the creation of special blood cells, which, in turn, release chemicals (histamines) that cause **inflammation** (redness, heat, swelling, pain). The purpose of the inflammation is to dilute and destroy the invading 'agent'.

immunised: protection from an infection/disease/**disorder** as a result of a previous attack or as a result of a **vaccine** (either natural or synthetic).

impairment: damage that interferes with the development of function/**ability**.

inflammation: an **immune system** reaction designed to dilute and destroy something that is threatening the body (e.g. infection, **allergen**, injury, harsh chemicals on the skin). Symptoms, which include redness, swelling, heat and pain, are caused by cells and fluid that gather at the site of the infection.

intellectual impairment (mental retardation/handicap): a pattern of persistently slow learning of basic skills during childhood, and a significantly below-normal intellectual **ability** as an adult.

intelligence: an indicator of how easy/difficult it will be for someone to learn. Some believe it can be measured, others think not.

in utero: in the uterus, before birth.

IQ test: first devised by Alfred Binet to describe the relationship between a person's real age and their mental/intellectual age (and whether they are typical of their peers, or better or worse).

maladaptive: behaviour that is contrary to normal expectations to the extent that it interferes negatively with all or many aspects of daily life.

midline, crossing: the **ability** to work in the left visual field with the right hand, or vice versa.

multi-disciplinary team: professionals who work together to evaluate a problem and/or work together to treat it (e.g. a programme involving speech therapy, medication and school learning support).

multi-sensory: presenting information using more than just one sense aims to meet the particular learning styles, preferences or strengths of the learners, based on the idea that not all children learn equally well in the same way.

neurological: refers to brain and nervous system functioning.

neurologist: a medical doctor who specialises in understanding and diagnosing the interaction between brain functioning, the nervous system and other body functions (e.g. muscle functioning).

neuron/e: a nerve cell, which sends and receives the messages that travel along nerves.

neuropsychology: studies brain and nervous system functioning and its effect on **cognition**, movement and behaviour.

nocturnal seizures (benign Rolandic epilepsy): a form of epilepsy characterised by primarily night-time **seizures** while the child is asleep (although in some children daytime seizures may also occur).

non-verbal intellectual ability: **ability** to learn from visual and motor information (seeing and doing) and to solve visual and motor problems.

norms: average or typical characteristics of a group of people which are used for comparisons with other groups to see how alike or different they are.

oro-motor: actions such as talking and sucking that involve the muscles of the mouth, tongue, face, throat, and so on.

otitis media: infections of the middle ear (see *MIDDLE EAR INFECTIONS, HEARING*).

personality disorder: maladaptive behaviour that is markedly different from the expectations of the individual's society, interfering in all aspects of life. Examples include obsessive-compulsive, dependent and inhibited **disorders**.

phobia: a strong, persistent fear that is out of proportion to the danger actually present, to the extent that a person cannot function properly when that fear is present.

phonics (English language phonics): matching sounds we hear in words to the letter symbols of the alphabet and to the letter combinations that are part of the rules of the English language (e.g. long 'a' sound matches with 'ai/ay/a-e'). Phonics exist in languages that have written forms.

seizure: abnormal and uncontrollable body sensations (e.g. drowsiness, nausea), movements (e.g. jerking, stumbling) and behaviours (e.g. verbal outbursts, strange noises, plucking at clothes).

self-advocacy: to understand yourself what you need to be successful, knowing and valuing yourself, planning, acting and learning from the outcomes of your actions.

self-esteem: a person's sense or feeling of self-worth and self-liking.

self-image: a person's mental or internal 'picture' of him/herself (e.g. physical appearance, their importance to others, how well they are liked).

significant: statistically speaking, this means that something is not very likely to have happened by chance and that it is therefore most probably true.

standardised: rules that have to be followed whenever an evaluation (e.g. an **IQ test**) takes place, to make sure that it is always administered in the same way, using the same procedures and the same comparisons, thus making it as fair as possible and leaving as little as possible to chance.

statistics: mathematical techniques that summarise numbers (e.g. scores on a test) to see what patterns, if any, emerge. Statistics try to determine what results might be due to chance and what might be due to a real effect (e.g. a lucky guess versus actual knowledge).

steroids: hormones that include the sex hormones (e.g. oestrogen, androgen) and **cortico-steroid**s produced by the adrenal gland.

syndrome: pattern of behaviours that indicate the presence of a **disorder**.

vaccine: a substance that stimulates the body's immune response; the goal of vaccination is to prevent infection. There are several different types of vaccines.

verbal intellectual ability: the **ability** to learn from verbal information and to demonstrate knowledge using verbal means.

verbal IQ: verbal **intelligence** as measured on an **IQ test**.

Index

Page references in *italics* indicate diagrams; those in **bold** refer to glossary entries